Implementing Total Quality Management in Higher Education

by

Robert Cornesky

Sam McCool

Larry Byrnes

Robert Weber

Library of Congress Cataloging-in-Publication Data

Implementing total quality management in higher education / by
    Robert Cornesky ... [et al.].
            p.   cm.
    Includes bibliographical references (p.   ).
    ISBN 0-912150-17-3   : $31.95
    1. Universities and colleges—United States—Administration.
    2. Total quality management—United States. I. Cornesky, Robert.
    LB2341.I4   1992
    978.73—dc20   92-9592
                                            CIP

Second Printing — 1992

Printed in the United States of America
Library of Congress Catalog Card Number: 92-9592
ISBN: 0-912150-17-3

Magna Publications, Inc.
2718 Dryden Dr.
Madison, WI 53704
(608) 246-3580

Contents

Acknowledgments

We cannot begin to acknowledge all of the faculty, staff, and administrators who have helped us and provided ideas on how to improve the quality of the educational experience. Still, two people in particular must be recognized for their contributions toward improving quality: Burton Witthuhn, provost and vice president for academic affairs at Western Illinois University, and Leo Goodman-Malamuth II, president of Governors State University.

Burt Witthuhn is a highly innovative thinker who constantly takes established ideas and improves upon them in quantum leaps. For example, in 1987 he originally had the idea of taking Dr. Deming's points and applying them to higher education. Burt always supports quality educational experiences.

Leo Goodman-Malamuth II personifies more than anyone we know Deming's fifth point: Improve constantly. Under Leo's leadership, Governors State University has emerged as an institution with unquestioned educational excellence.

R.C.

Introduction

Problems in American higher education can be directly attributed to the lack of vision, the lack of insight, and the lack of skill of many administrators who lacked any formal, even informal, management training. During the rapid growth of higher education in the 1960s and 1970s, unskilled or inefficient managers set the stage for long-term problems associated with planning and development, budget management, personnel administration, and the perceived decline in quality among university graduates.

Examples of the lack of quality range from outmoded instructional techniques, poorly prepared professionals, and mounting calls for the reform of professional and teacher preparation. Other examples include demands for restructuring professional and general education programs, streamlining budgets, and improving the quality of incoming students. Clearly, there is growing unrest about the quality of higher education at federal, state, and local levels of government and education.

Traditionally there has always been a fear of changing the systems by which value or worth are measured. Only when change has been forced by the need to survive have institutions, like industry, banking, government, and education, discovered new ways to measure worth. Measuring the worth of objects or systems is an extension of projecting self-worth. To change the perspective challenges individual perceptions of worth.

Inherited self-worth is the hardest notion to change, simply because it is usually the hardest thing for an individual to examine objectively. It follows that institutions, which in many cases are structured on value systems that protect individuals from having to confront questions of worth, value, and quality, are the least likely to change. Even when change is needed, or the need for change is recognized or expected, actually changing the institution remains a difficult process. There is an irony in that industry has been conditioned to expect innovation to come from universities, despite the lack of change and leadership academic institutions have traditionally shown.

The trouble with higher education is, by and large, **not** with the preparation, ability and commitment of its professors. Rather, the trouble is more directly attributable to the lack of administrative leadership from school presidents, vice presidents, deans, and to some extent, the chairpersons and the governing boards. Major responsibility must be placed first on these administrators, since many have yielded to the pressures of the present rather than making a commitment to quality while looking toward and preparing for the future. Industries, including corporations, school districts, and hospitals, also share the blame for hiring ill-prepared graduates and not demanding better quality.

Blame is not a good word from our perspective. There is no blame here; rather it is the acknowledgement of a system that is dysfunctional since it is based on fear. Administrators without leadership qualities or visionary ability generally yield to their fear of the unknown when confronted with change. They lack a sense of adventure; they distrust imagination. Faced with change or conflict, they are sometimes forced to deal with it in non-productive, defensive ways. Usually, the defensive systems they use reflect their own educational experiences. Naturally, they fall back on this conservative, defensive style as one would reflexively respond to a punch by raising an arm and flinching. What we propose instead, to carry the analogy through, is effective leadership that responds to change as a jujitsu artist would, by grabbing the "punch," transforming it into a throw, and thereby gaining the advantage.

In his publication *Higher Education and the Public Interest: A Report to the Campus,* Gary H. Quehl (1988, p. 1) pointed out: *There is a major erosion of confidence in the leadership and the quality of higher education in the country. Respect for colleges and universities is gravely in danger.* Rightly so! Lack of leadership in the nation's colleges and universities brought on this problem, which resulted in administrators making colleges and universities respond to the instant gratification needs of individuals, rather than **leading and directing** them to respond to the nation's future needs. Short-sighted administrators controlled the system, and it responded appropriately by guiding the public into a status quo position!

Furthermore, it is difficult for a system threatened on all sides and forced to adopt a defensive mode to improve quality. Protecting themselves from criticism and cost-cutting efforts by state legislators, college and university administrators are not going to root out what is wrong with their systems. They have diverted their attention from their main purpose — producing a quality education — to maintaining the status quo. Lacking imagination or creativity, they cannot respond to outside criticism with innovative systems, but instead fall prey to manipulation and ineptitude.

Administrators can effect meaningful change over the next several decades by instituting a total quality management (TQM) philosophy as a process for guiding colleges and universities toward total quality improvement (TQI). If institutions of higher education follow the points of the quality gurus, like W. Edwards Deming, Philip Crosby, Joseph Juran, and Masaaki Imai, they will have:

- constructive competition;
- shared values and unity of purpose;
- collaboration on broad issues;
- simultaneous and synergistic planning;
- emphasis on responsibility to contribute;
- decentralized partnerships built upon situational management;
- team accountability;
- constancy of purpose;
- win-win resolution to conflicts via conflict management;
- and probably most important, a superior professorate, student body, and administration.

In summary, organizational cultures will be transformed.

Our basic premise is that institutions of higher education should plan more effectively, especially in regard to utilizing resources. We stress the concept of self-evaluation rather than self-protection. We urge the rooting out of **fat** and inefficiency. We urge a collaborative approach recognizing the value of input from all quarters, and to ensure quality, we urge administrators to establish total quality management processes.

The cost of higher education increases significantly with poor management. When college was the exclusive province of a small portion of society, when college enrollments were manageable and predictable, when a small support staff was sufficient to maintain records and handle the routines of scheduling and monitoring student progress, and when the idea of faculty belonging to a union would have been cause for derision, it must have been relatively easy to manage and to fund administrative operations.

For those who work in higher education in an environment where computer operation centers employ more people than some departments, where administrative staff members are necessary to attend to contractual issues, where support staff members are employed to teach remedial courses, and where forms exist for everything, it is understandable that many, particularly faculty, see an ongoing proliferation of administrators and support staff to the detriment of the institution's primary educational mission. Commentary on the size of the administrative budget compared to the academic budget five, 10 or 20 years ago reinforces the prevailing view on most college campuses that expenses have gotten out of hand.

Aside from positions and offices that have been established on campuses in response to pressing social issues, it is clear that one of the most pronounced growth areas in administrative staff at both the local campus level and the system level has been with administering collective bargaining agreements.

It is not our intention to argue for or against collective bargaining agreements. What we are focusing on is the cost associated with decisions and how decisions often lead to the establishment of a far more complex and expensive proposition than that which surrounded the initial problem.

Case Study: The Price of Doing Business

At mid-sized state colleges, designated by the state legislature as universities in the mid-1970s, a revenue shortfall resulted in a call-back of a certain portion of each system school's previously apportioned budget. Immediately the flagship state university raised a storm of protest, enlisted the support of state legislators and alumni, and mounted a campaign in the media to denounce the budget cuts. So strong were their efforts and so consistent was the university's media support that the state legislature quickly gave in and announced a much lower callback for the flagship university than for the remaining schools in the system. **System priorities** was the catch phrase.

Individual legislators lobbied as best they could for their local schools, but they were no match for the organized strength of the flagship university, which also was conveniently located in the state capital, allowing for even more informal pressure to be placed on the assembled legislators. Since this was the period of rabid student unrest associated with the war in Viet Nam, the legislators wanted as little controversy as possible.

The schools in the state system had undergone a rapid period of change in the mid-1960s. From single-purpose teacher training colleges, they were transformed almost overnight to multi-purpose state colleges, and when they had all somehow at the same magic moment achieved university level, the state legislature granted them university status. What that seemed to mean on most system campuses was growth. Unlimited growth. The more students the school admitted, the more funds they would receive in next year's budget allocation.

A pattern began to emerge. Growth meant admitting large numbers of students, who a short time prior to this period would not have been eligible for admission. Growth meant petitioning the system office for new degrees since faculty were busy inventing new courses, new concentrations, and new programs.

Throughout the state enrollments boomed. Local state legislators pointed with pride at the local campus. Everybody took credit for the expansion. The president usually had a newly completed student center or athletic facility named after him (there were few female presidents at that time). The local politician campaigning for re-election would stress the amount of state funds that had been directed into the local campus, thereby benefiting the entire local economy. Parents of the new students could point with pride at their offspring now at the local school majoring in business or education. To some it was the fulfillment of the American dream at last with higher education representing the cornerstone of that promise.

But who were these new students and were they really ready and suited for college? Older faculty began grousing about the erosion of standards. Remedial courses found their way into the curriculum for the first time. Burgeoning enrollments resulted in tremendous difficulty in finding adequate, qualified faculty. System schools found the demand so intense that they would hire freshman English instructors and basic math teachers over the phone, dispensing with the more conventional approach of a search and screen process. Students who had recently completed degrees soon found themselves coaxed into college teaching paths by faculty and administrators, who, intent upon filling their lower level teaching slots, urged them to enroll in their newly established masters programs. Local high school teachers, most of whom had graduated from the local school and had obtained their masters in education at the same school by going part-time over a number of years, were brought in to fill whatever vacancy existed.

Given such staffing patterns the old notion of gaining tenure was soon replaced by a sort of automatic tenure after a period of years. Some departments were so large that faculty were tenured without completing terminal degrees, without publications, or without significant service of any sort.

Growth meant that every year the state legislature would be pressed for new revenue-generating taxes. Inevitably a backlash occurred. Taxpayers, even though they recognized that their son or daughter was receiving a college education that they never had, grew resentful. Enough was enough. Tax revolt was in the air. Something had to be done.

The announcement of a fiscal crisis was treated by the state media as a relief to the mounting pressure for a halt to ever-increasing taxes. The average person revealed unanimous support for controlling spending, yet those same taxpayers were seldom asked just what they would like to see cut or controlled.

When the legislature announced its solution to the budget crisis, including the rollback policy for higher education, few complaints were heard.

In reviewing this situation from a quality standpoint it is clear the administration failed to understand its obligations and failed in carrying out its primary purpose. They chose, for whatever reasons, a shortsighted approach designed to produce the smallest fallout rather than seek a solution that would not only meet the demands of the situation but prevent overspending in the future. There was no enrollment analysis, no conception of what programs and degrees should be offered. This was an administration chosen for its degree of loyalty to growth at all costs. Lower-level administrators were rewarded with upper-level positions if they contributed to growth.

An administration so infiltrated with the wrong message could not be committed to quality. The quality of instructional programs and the quality of the delivery of instructional services were not in the forefront of their minds as they grappled for the first time with a deficit situation. For the most part these administrators had no experience other than at the very institution they were running.

This was an administration set apart from the faculty and removed from students. They signed the papers that hired and promoted faculty, awarded raises, and granted tenure. But, there was no interaction between faculty and administration. The orientation of new faculty was a cursory exercise designed to put fear of continuation in the minds of those without doctorates. This was not a caring administration which looked to the future by grooming young instructors; this was not an administration which spoke with faculty about curriculum development, grant opportunities, or personal development. This was an administration marked by its indifference to the very role it was supposed to fill.

Inefficient and uncaring administrators set into motion long term consequences of their often inappropriate actions. It is a system that forces administrators at one institution to guarantee summer contracts even if no students enroll, and at another institution forces the administration to award sabbaticals to persons who have already retired. These absurdities are passed off as the price that must be paid for past inefficiencies, yet they are also the price that will continue to be paid until a change in the institutional culture occurs. This price, which in our estimation is 40 percent fat, is the price for doing business in colleges and universities!

Before management begins to analyze the "fat" within their institution of higher education, they should undertake an effort to establish total quality management (TQM) processes. This can only be done by having all of the top mangers trained in TQM processes and systems, and then to actively establish the processes and systems throughout the entire institution. TQM, unlike successful planning and resource allocation procedures, must come from the top down — from the president to the deans to the faculty and staff — to the student.

As the chief executive officer (CEO) and the chief academic officer (CAO) make it known that TQM is to be applied to the work place, management should begin an educational calibration process to train everyone in the institution. The educational endeavors should contain discussions on the processes and systems leading to total quality improvement. These educational workshops, once established, should be ongoing as to reinforce the commitment to quality.

Chapter 1:
Approaches to Total Quality Management

The purpose of this chapter is to introduce readers to the principles of total quality management (TQM) by briefly (1) reviewing the ideas of TQM leaders, and (2) discussing how their ideas might apply to institutions of higher education.

The Deming Approach

Of all of the people known for stressing quality, W. Edwards Deming is the pioneer. He stresses statistical process control (SPC) and a 14-point process for managers to improve quality and productivity. Deming's approach is humanistic, and treats people as intelligent human beings who want to do a good job. Deming "hates" managers who allege that workers are responsible for quality problems.

After convincing and encouraging Japan's top mangers to produce quality items for Western consumption by using SPC and his 14-point process, the Japanese were exporting quality goods within five years. Japan, recognizing Deming's contribution to its economy, instituted the annual Deming Prize for contributions to quality of a product and/or service. In 1960, Japan's Emperor awarded Deming the Second Order Medal of Sacred Treasure.

Deming's 14 points (1986, p. 23) follow:

1. *Create constancy of purpose for improvement of product and service, with the aim of becoming competitive and staying in business, and to provide jobs.*

2. *Adopt the new philosophy. We are in a new economic age. Western management must awaken to the challenge, learn their responsibilities, and take on leadership for change.*

3. *Cease dependence on inspection to achieve quality. Eliminate the need for inspection on a mass basis by building quality into the product in the first place.*

4. *End the practice of awarding business on the basis of price tag alone. Move toward a single supplier for any one item on the basis of a long-term relationship of loyalty and trust. Minimize total cost by working with a single supplier.*

5. *Improve constantly and forever every process for planning, production, and service, to improve quality and productivity, and thus constantly decrease costs.*

6. *Institute training on the job.*

7. *Adopt and institute leadership. The aim of supervision should be to help people and machines and gadgets do a better job. Supervision of management is in need of overhaul, as well as supervision of production workers.*

8. *Drive out fear, so that everyone can work effectively for the company.*

9. *Break down barriers between departments. People in research, design, sales, and production must work as a team to foresee problems of production and those that may be encountered with the product or service.*

10. *Eliminate slogans, exhortations, and targets for the work force that ask for zero defects or new levels of productivity. Such exhortations only create adversarial relationships, since the bulk of the causes of low quality and productivity belong to the system and thus lie beyond the power of the work force.*

11 a. *Eliminate work standards (quotas) on the factory floor. Substitute leadership.*

   b. *Eliminate management by objectives. Eliminate management by numbers, and numerical goals. Substitute leadership.*

12 a. *Remove barriers that rob the hourly worker of his right to pride of workmanship. The responsibility of supervisors must be changed from sheer numbers to quality.*

   b. *Remove barriers that rob people in management and engineering of their right to pride of workmanship. This means, inter alia, abolishment of the annual or merit rating and of management by objective.*

13. *Institute a vigorous program of education and self-improvement.*

14. *Put everybody in the company to work to accomplish the transformation. The transformation is everybody's job.*

Let us briefly examine each of the points and consider how they might be applied to institutions of higher education. For a more complete discussion of Deming's philosophy and how it might be applied to higher education, please refer to Cornesky et al. (1990).

Point 1: Create a Constancy of Purpose

Most academic institutions have ill-defined and confusing mission statements. Some mission statements are totally misleading, whereas others are so comprehensive that they are meaningless. Faculty and administration need to utilize research data and jointly produce a plan which concentrates on a focused mission statement that is responsive to present and projected societal trends and needs, and realistic for the institution and its budget. Regardless of the institution, the mission statement should incorporate innovative teaching and learning strategies, and have a total quality improvement (TQI) oriented philosophy.

Point 2: Adopt the New Philosophy

Once the institution's focused mission is in place, the president and governing board must accept the plan. We do not mean "accept" as in to receive (in agreement), but rather as in embracing or taking on as guiding policy. Then the president must get the vice presidents, deans, and faculty involved in adopting the plan. Only when the top management seriously adopts a plan based on quality, trust, and pride of workmanship will it be accepted by the faculty, staff, and students.

After the quality-based philosophy is accepted, the administration and faculty must introduce new terminal competencies for all students to assure the public that new graduates will have the capacity to initiate and respond to change, and to cooperate for the good of society as a whole. If the TQI philosophy is adopted, newly empowered staff, alumni, students, faculty, and administrators will discuss aspects of every day events that detract from the quality of education: repeated careless mistakes, poor policies, antiquated equipment, vague directions, poor professional development plans, failure to respond to change, and poor supervision. This is but one way to encourage collegiality, change attitudes and behavior, and establish a "culture" that seeks to establish quality.

In his recent evaluation of the state of education, *The Quality School*, Dr. William Glasser (1990, p. 425-435) says public schools are not properly managed, and that the only high-quality educational experiences offered to students are athletics, music, drama and a few advanced placement courses. He believes that less that 15 percent of students do high-quality work. He compares teachers with industrial managers and students with workers, and uses an analogy of Deming when he suggests that the success of the students (workers) is directly related to how they are managed by the teachers, and correlates the success of the teachers directly to the upper-level supervisors. In fact, Dr. Glasser states *an effective teacher is one who is able to convince not one-half or three-quarters but essentially all of his or her students to do high quality work in school.*

Point 3: Cease Dependency on Inspection to Achieve Quality

In the university setting, Deming's third point applies to selecting students, and to a lesser degree, selecting all employees, including faculty and administrators. Ideally, colleges or universities only admit students who have the necessary skills to do college-level work. Thus "perceived" quality would be built into the program during the freshman year. Many private institutions and select public institutions have rigid admission criteria, and their students, for the most part, would be able to survive and thrive in any institution, including outdated, rigid educational systems, as well as highly innovative educational systems.

A primary goal of public institutions is to provide a quality education to a maximum number of people at a reasonable cost. Although colleges and universities have different missions and different entrance requirements, many still use selection criteria that are archaic, socially and racially biased, and non-responsive to the present and future needs of the country. We recommend that public institutions critically examine their student selection process and consider using a variety of newer methods rather than the traditional criteria. This does not necessarily mean that quality cannot be built into the freshman selection. The selection process should be designed to involve students, alumni, faculty, administration, and future employers.

To better judge the "quality" (skills) of incoming students, we think it is important that the faculty and administration establish a long-term, close, working relationship with the school districts and community colleges from which they select most of their students. By having a close, personal, working relationship with and by clearly defining entrance requirements for incoming high school and community college graduates, the university can expect closer cooperation by working with counselors alone.

We recommend that colleges and universities establish a system for random student testing in every course. The testing should be done by outside evaluators and should be constructed to evaluate faculty and students as they relate to the blueprint in which they are working and the long-range plan and mission of the institution. Under no circumstances do we recommend standardized state-wide exams for comparing students or teachers or institutions. We recommend that institutions of higher education capitalize on the areas in which students have excelled while in grades K-12, and seek to develop these skills further: this is one way quality can be built into the very beginning of the educational process.

We recommend that all institutions make greater use of non-graded, interdisciplinary courses for general education. We also suggest that student learning styles and professors' teaching styles be assessed, and that students be placed in classes where teaching and learning styles are compatible. We encourage institutions to experiment with different teaching methods to meet the educational needs of minorities, since the present system does not (and never did) do a satisfactory job of educating minorities. We also recommend that **faculty utilize cooperative learning** so students can **gain skills necessary to succeed in the work place**. Of course, good advising, good counseling, good mentoring, good cooperative education opportunities, and a good freshman orientation experience are key elements in building a quality education.

In promoting the Deming philosophy, Glasser (1990, p. 429) states that the trouble with teachers being required to teach toward measurable fragments of knowledge is that students and teachers both know this has nothing to do with a high-quality education. In fact, Glasser implies that standardized tests ensure a low-quality fragmented approach to teaching and learning. Both Glasser and Deming point out that inspecting (testing) does not build in quality.

Point 4: Stop Doing Business on the Basis of Price Alone

Universities need to limit bidding processes by writing locked-in specifications when a given quality for certain equipment and/or supplies is required. This will permit the institution to work with certain suppliers to establish a long-term relationship — one in which the supplier, after becoming aware of the institution's mission, will promote and support the institution.

Point 5: Improve Constantly

If quality is to become part of an institution's culture, everyone, including the faculty, staff, and administration, must improve efficiency and become responsive to the needs of students. All employees must consider themselves unique, and every student must be considered unique. Ideally every employee should be a mentor to a student as every upper-division student should be a mentor to either a lower-division student or to a student in K-12. If quality is going to improve constantly, all employees should have access to institutional research data, which should include answers to such questions as: Who are our graduates? Where do they work? What do employers think of our graduates? How have the educational experiences at our institution changed the alumni? Once these answers are known, then everyone in the institution can ask: **How can I do a better job for our graduates?** Toward this end, we encourage administration to ask constantly of every employee: What have you changed today that will help us improve the quality of our graduates?

Point 6: Institute On-The-Job Training

We encourage academic institutions to immerse new employees in **training programs** so they quickly understand and accept the school's "common language" and "culture." This also includes part-time, temporary employees.

Most colleges and universities hire secretaries, custodians, faculty, and administrators without clearly identifying job expectations, institutional philosophy and mission, or administrative objectives. In short, orientation programs for new employees are often poorly executed or nonexistent. Many employees must establish their own criteria for doing a perceived "good" job, whereas in fact their supervisors rate them poorly.

The consequences of not having an orientation program include the hiring of a vice president of development who actively seeks to raise funds but does not enlist the assistance and advice of the faculty and staff, or a vice president of finance who determines the distribution of the budget but does not enlist the assistance and advice of the faculty and staff. To make matters worse, when employees are asked to participate in the aforesaid activities, they are not educated on their expected roles, and everyone ends up doing "her/his own thing," which may or may not contribute to the mission of the institution, and may even detract from a quality education.

Ideally, every university or college employee should be able to help students seeking advice. Employees should be educated thoroughly on the policies, procedures, and culture of the institution as well as the specifics of her or his particular job. All administrative and staff employees should realize that it is their function to **serve** the faculty, and all faculty members should realize that their function is to **serve** the students, which will in turn benefit society. Ideally, employees would feel part of a team, and as a result, everyone would have pride in her or his work. This "ideal" may not be obtainable in a complex organization such as a college or university, but it is not even approachable without training on the job.

Point 7: Improve Leadership

Deming's seventh point is the keystone that holds and supports the entire philosophy to ensure success. Without leadership, institutions of higher education can only talk about quality, change, innovation, and service.

The following examples illustrate the results of unprepared graduates, caused by inadequate leadership in colleges and universities:

- A student who flunks out of college at the end of the first year is discovered to be deficient in basic reading and writing skills. The professors blame either the recruiting office for admitting the student or the high school for passing the student without certain basic competencies having been met. The high school teachers and administrators blame the elementary schools. The elementary schools blame the parents for not insisting that their children do the necessary homework.

- An American business firm fails because it cannot compete with foreign manufacturers. Another large business has to spend millions of dollars every year to re-educate college graduates in the skills they should have obtained as part of a standard curriculum.

Most of the responsibility for these failures falls squarely on the shoulders of college administrators. Within the past several decades, for example, institutions of higher education have graduated education majors who are inadequately prepared to meet the challenges facing them in the classroom. They graduated school administrators who are not fully prepared to assist teachers in meeting these challenges, and who either pressure teachers to pass students who are not qualified, or pressure teachers to conform to the "traditional" methods of teaching and testing. Schools of business teach finance, banking, and marketing using an ethic based on instant gratification, rather than quality and long-term societal gain. Professional schools of law and medicine also adhere to the instant gratification syndrome.

To establish a greater possibility of hiring leaders with vision and innovative ideas, test all potential administrators to identify these traits. Administrators must demonstrate a spirit of achievement, while recognizing that organizational excellence is based on innovation, committed people, and the care of students. Administrators should be

21

vision-oriented, creative change agents who can express their visions to the faculty. If administrators have the leadership abilities to relate an inspiring vision to the faculty, and if they lead by example and practice visible management, the faculty and staff will respond quickly by embracing TQI as a means of improving the quality of education.

A central theme stated by Marilyn Ferguson (1980) and Tom Peters (1988) is that effective leaders embrace new ideas and challenge old ones. For ideas to become part of an actively pursued vision, however, collegiality must exist between the faculty, administration and staff. Everyone must cooperate, continually point out failures in the "system," and try to improve daily, even if in incremental amounts, the quality of teaching, advising, service, and responsiveness of the system. There should be continuous performance assessments as they relate to processes and systems, as improvement will occur only when everyone is capable of taking risks without the fear of failing. If collegiality exists, and it can exist only under enlightened leadership, a decentralization of the entire university or college would result, causing everyone to adopt an attitude of situational leadership where the power to act is based upon competencies, rather than title or rank. Of course there would be instances of failure and confusion, but if the leader's vision is clear and if the change toward TQI is demanded, an internal adjustment would quickly be made, and no one in the organization would be afraid to reach his or her potential.

A vision promoting TQI, therefore, has to be firmly directed from the top and be articulated clearly and frequently. Administrators have to understand that teaching fewer students well is more important than teaching a large number poorly. The faculty have to understand that they are expected to take bold initiatives in teaching, advising, creative activities, and service. Such a vision is possible and can be implemented, but leaders must first challenge faculty to do it.

Glasser (1990) recommends empowering teachers *and* students in the process of establishing quality. To do this requires powerful leadership.

In order for the faculty to take on this challenge, however, administrators must manage by example. They must constantly ask how procedures and processes have been changed to improve quality. To stay current, managers must circulate among the faculty and staff for *more than one-third of the time* (Peters 1988, p. 510).

Point 8: Drive Out Fear

Fear must be removed from the work setting so employees can work constructively. Administrators may want to accomplish this by establishing trust through positioning and confidence through respect. When employees feel they are trusted, they will take more pride in their work and quality will improve. As quality improves, the work place will become a fun place, rather that just a job. A fun place develops and promotes collegiality, and the cycle starts all over again.

Trust through positioning and confidence through respect, coupled with a clear vision, alone will not "drive out fear." Faculty and staff must be involved actively in planning the future of the institution. Peters (1988, p. 615) points out that *a good strategic planning process (1) gets everyone involved, (2) is not constrained by overall corporate 'assumptions...' (3) is perpetually fresh, forcing the asking of new questions, (4) is not left to planners, and (5) requires lots of noodling time and vigorous debate. As for the document per se, it (1) is succinct, (2) emphasizes the development of strategic skills, and (3) is burned the day before it goes to the printer —that is, it is a living document, not an icon.* If this type of planning takes place, fear will be headed out the door and an air of cooperation will begin to intervene.

Bottom-up planning does not suggest that top management should not assess the reality of the plan; it suggests that top management not act without knowing the capabilities of the faculty and staff who must execute the plan.

Both the administration and the faculty must actively modify the master plan every year or two to maintain the right course toward the future.

Two things must be either modified or eliminated from the master plan if fear is to be reduced and if the organization will improve significantly: (1) management by objectives (MBO) and (2) job descriptions.

MBO, according to Peters (1988, p. 603) *is one more great idea that has been neutered by bureaucrats in nine out of 10 applications. That is, MBO (like performance appraisals) is a superb tool if the objectives are (1) simple, (2) focused on what's important, (3) genuinely created from the bottom up (the objectives are drafted by the person who must live up to them, with no constraining guides), and (4) a 'living' contract, not a form-driven exercise.*

Job descriptions tend to tie people down to narrow functions, and are often favored by people who prefer paper over people (Peters 1988, p. 605). Job descriptions not only do not favor situational management, they also reduce the possibility of having pride in workmanship. Job descriptions favor centralization of authority, information, planning and resource allocation — all of which instill fear, rather than driving fear out. Finally, job descriptions increase barriers between departments, rather than breaking them down.

Case Study: Drive in Fear and Change the Culture

The amount of time and effort spent by colleges and universities in filling vacancies, particularly at the senior management level, has in some cases reached a point of absurdity. In what should be a straightforward search for the best qualified candidate, institutions find themselves beset by a bewildering variety of problems, not all of which are designed to ensure the hiring of the best qualified person.

A case in point focuses on the filling of administrative positions at a mid-sized, Northeastern state college. The institutional culture within this organization was marked by cynicism and open mistrust of administrators by members of the faculty. The faculty had organized into a union, but instead of insisting on a voice in the hiring of those who would serve in upper level management positions, the local union took the highly unusual stance of refusing to nominate anyone for search committees other than for faculty slots.

The union's rationale was that teaching was faculty work and administration was not faculty work. Therefore, in their wisdom, the two would never cross. Not all faculty agreed with that viewpoint, but as often happens on unionized campuses, it was difficult if not impossible for a minority view to surface into action. The purpose of the union, after all, was to speak for the majority of the membership.

Even when the union was expressly asked by the president or the board of trustees to participate in searches, it steadfastly held by its separation of powers or duties. Thus, management-level vacancies, from dean to president, were filled without any faculty involvement. Each new president, dean, or vice president simply fit into the local scheme of things for a period of years and then left or retired. Certain union leaders were convinced that these people were sent by God as punishment for their sins and would eventually leave, so at the very least they must be tolerated.

A new president decided that he was going to change the institutional culture. Upon arriving on campus he immediately went to what he correctly perceived the roots of power at the institution — the union leadership. He granted 75 percent release time to both the president and vice president of the union. No one seemed to question the granting of state funds for such purposes. He also made it a rule to consult with the union leadership at least once a week. As time progressed, the union leadership found itself welcome in the president's office. He broke down barriers between the departments (see Deming's ninth point, below). However, it became apparent to the deans and vice presidents that the union leaders were informed on major issues before they were.

Grievances which once flowed from the union office stopped. The new president would point with pride to the fact that in the past year not a single grievance left the local campus, as everything was resolved at the local level. It was obvious that the union leadership was happy with the president. Yet, deans began to grumble as they were being overruled at every turn. If a dean said no to a two-day-a-week schedule, he would be overturned by a vice president or the president. If a dean said no to any faculty member, it was clear that the president would be approachable and agreeable.

The president was proud about how he changed the institutional culture. He insisted he would not tolerate anyone trying to change the "new" culture and that he would destroy any manager who fought against it. People either agreed with the president or they were out of the power structure; not out of a job, however, for this was a president who could not bring himself to fire people. Rather, unfortunate managers would find that meetings were held on topics that should have included them or their immediate supervisor would order them to perform tasks clearly of a lower echelon than what that person should have been doing.

Eventually, by driving fear into the system, the president drove out quality. By establishing trust and communication with only a select group and excluding others, he created a "new" culture, exemplified by the applaudable reduction of grievances, but still lacking in collegial trust and pride, still incapable of establishing cooperation among administrators, faculty, and staff. The union leadership and the faculty still would not participate in the selection of administrators, in spite of all of the concessions made by the president!

Point 9: Break Down Barriers Between Departments

Central to breaking down all barriers are (1) a sense of belonging, (2) meaningful communication, and (3) integrity in dealings.

Peters (1988, p. 627) corroborates this quality point and connects it to flexibility and innovation: *Quality and flexibility —and constant innovation —are chief among the new winner's watchwords. These traits require wholesale involvement by the employees and a willingness to work together. Barriers between functions must fall, as must adversarial relations between labor and management... Involvement by all and non-adversarial relations must rest on a cornerstone of trust, which in turn can only be engendered by total integrity.*

A sense of belonging should be established by the open sharing of information, such as all institutional data, and by involving all employees in such activities as a capital fund drive. These activities require encouraging employees to be innovative and flexible. Barriers inhibit innovation, and selective communication and trust, as seen above, prevent flexibility and cooperation. Administrators must create a culture in which trust breaks down barriers, and that involves employees in the whole system.

In instituting meaning through communication, administrators must not differentiate between staff members and members of the governing board — information and concerns should be shared openly. We also suggest that administrators deal with the employees consistently, with trust and integrity.

Point 10:   Replace Slogans, Exhortations and Targets with Methods that Work

Slogans like, "Let's improve the quality of our graduates," are ineffectual. The slogan implies that the faculty can produce a better qualified graduate even though the students they start with are incapable of either reading or writing at the college level. Slogans can be harmful if the quality of students is marginal or if equipment is broken, since faculty members are expected to perform in an unstable system — a system they have no control over. Unless all employees actively participate in improving the system, quality slogans have no connection with reality. Indeed, managers who promote slogans but do not follow with action are hypocritical. Hypocrisy becomes the enemy, since *The boss who preaches quality... is seen as a hypocrite* (Peters 1988, p. 631).

Point 11:   Eliminate Quotas and Numerical Goals —
           Substitute Leadership

Deming believes that quotas and numerical goals impede quality more than any other single working condition. Yet, entire state systems are funded on student enrollments and other items such as the size of the physical plant. Within a given institution, the budget may be allocated to the academic departments based entirely on the student credit hours generated, rather than the quality of the graduate. A budget based solely on the size of the student body and the number of student credit hours generated encourages colleges and universities to accept students who are not prepared for the college experience. Such budgeting may even encourage faculty to grade "easier" to ensure a sufficient enrollment to maintain a current faculty level, rather than risk the department's allocation. Imposed quotas and numerical work standards do as much as anything else to discourage collegiality.

Case Study: You Get Paid Even if no Students Take Your Class

A collective bargaining agreement stipulates that 90 percent of all summer school course offerings be guaranteed regardless of student enrollment. These are called firm contracts for which faculty receive payment regardless of enrollment. Indeed, professors have been known to receive full pay for courses which had no students! In addition, the first submission of courses does not include faculty names. Supposedly, this is done so initial selections are done objectively to avoid politicization of the process. Of course, department chairs, in order to develop schedules, know who is available to teach in the summer. They also know faculties' areas of expertise. In any case, they know who is scheduled to teach even though names are not submitted.

Most of the deliberations are not focused on the quality of the course offerings; rather, it is on selecting courses with appropriate credit hours to meet the requirement of the 90 percent firm and 10 percent contingency contracts. This is clearly a case where numerical quotas and goals, which mandate firm courses with guaranteed payment, discourage quality offerings and service to the students.

Point 12:   Remove Barriers that Rob
           Employees of their Right To Pride

This point deals with **removing barriers to pride of workmanship**, including the bureaucratic MBO and annual merit rating. Too many objectives are set by management and are numerically driven, rather than quality driven. Too many performance evaluations are numerically driven. In addition to being statistically invalid, they are used to threaten employees with no merit raise, when all too often merit pay is distributed to the "good old personal and cooperative friend" of the supervisor(s). Unless objectives and performance standards are defined clearly and measured frequently, using statistically valid multiple evaluation tools, and unless recognized deficiencies are tied directly into a development program, they reduce teaming and increase the "pleasing the boss" mentality.

Universities and colleges are complex organizations, and according to Hrebiniak (1978, p. 9), *every organization is an open system with respect to its environment. It engages in exchange with elements of its environment — suppliers, governmental regulatory agencies, customers, unions, and the like — to attain necessary inputs and dispose of outputs. It somehow transforms inputs into outputs. It interacts and bargains with external constituents as it defines goals and directions important for its future.*

It does not take a great deal of imagination to relate this definition of an open system to an institution of higher education.

As an open system, a college or university is cyclical; that is, students enter, are processed, and leave while the academy is influenced constantly by a variety of environmental factors. Since it is an open system, the college or university must constantly renew itself if it is to survive (Hrebiniak 1978, p. 10). A result of this pattern is that people tend to migrate toward disorganization, and complex physical systems tend to move from a patterned structure to a random distribution (Katz and Kahn 1966, p. 21). Therefore, to evaluate faculty members and the processes and systems in which they operate, a closed system within the open system must be established if faculty members are not to be confined in their development and if the processes and systems are to be improved. For example, the evaluation of faculty teaching must be treated as a closed system which has certainty and continuity. In the closed system, student, peer, administrative, and self-evaluations must be predictable. Evaluation in the closed system must be certain and constructive so that the professors' level of teaching and creativity, which occur in the open system, are not disturbed. With these thoughts in mind, Cornesky et al. (1990, p. 91) recommend a system for evaluating faculty — a system which, if done constructively and if tied directly to a professional development plan, could also drive out fear, promote cooperation, and increase innovation. One thing that should **never** be done, however, is to evaluate a professor on the basis of how well his or her students do on standardized exams.

Point 13: Institute a Vigorous Program of Education and Self-Improvement

With regard to Point 13, Walton (1984, p. 84) states *it is not enough to have good people in your organization. They must be continually acquiring the new knowledge and the new skills that are required to deal with new materials and new methods of production. Education and retraining — an investment in people — are required for long-term planning.*

The same holds true for colleges and universities: they must constantly educate and provide for professional and personal development if they are to stay current in the knowledge and skills required to prepare educated graduates — their only product.

Point 14: Involve Everyone in the Transformation to Quality

Deming's last point is to involve everyone in the transformation to quality. Too often, faculty and staff contributions are not sought, or they are ignored. Too many times the managers in institutions of higher education act as if they know all the answers to the everyday problems and, as a result, proceed to give orders and become boss-like, rather than accepting the fact that a brain comes with each body employed by the institution.

Five Deadly Diseases

Although some say Deming's philosophy cannot be applied to universities or colleges, we believe it can. It takes a commitment from the administration and a group of administrators, faculty, and staff willing to initiate these points. The result will be institutions of higher education which practice TQM and TQI and increasingly benefit society.

Like many American industries, institutions of higher education suffer from the "Deadly Diseases" and "Obstacles" as described by Deming (1982, p. 97). They are:

1. *Lack of constancy of purpose.*
2. *Emphasis on short-term results.*
3. *Evaluation of performance, merit rating, or annual review.*
4. *Mobility of top management.*

5.   *Running an institution on visible figures alone.*

Let us consider each of these diseases.

Disease 1: Lack of constancy of purpose

Most colleges and universities have mission statements that the faculty and staff have never read. Mission statements usually have not been updated for years, and if they have, they have not been tied into a long-range plan. If a long-range plan exists, it most likely:

- Was constructed by the upper administration without any meaningful input from the faculty and staff — the individuals responsible for carrying out the action objectives.

- Is sitting on a shelf without constant review or updating.

- Does not contain the input from the consumers (employers) of the product (graduates).

- Is not tied into a resource allocation plan to achieve the action objectives.

- Does not encourage innovation.

- Does not mention quality and does not have the full support of all the administration and faculty.

Most long-range plans and mission statements of colleges and universities are so broad and general that they are meaningless, especially if resources are not sufficient to accomplish the stated objectives. In fact, many comprehensive institutions act as if they are research universities offering doctorates, when in fact they simply do a good job in teaching and, at best, mediocre research.

Disease 2: Emphasis on short-term results

Many university employees hope only to survive the day. This includes secretaries, faculty, chairpersons, deans, vice presidents, and presidents. Some employees consider long-term results to be those expected by next week, rarely next month, almost never next year. Faculty have to concentrate on heavy teaching loads; administration on the required paper work. No one has time to understand what is happening in the other units, and most importantly, **no one has the time to point out faults in the processes and systems**. If faults are discovered, tradition and habit will usually dictate temporary repair, and then it is business as usual — no change toward TQI.

Students are admitted and processed. For the average public institution, 40 to 50 percent of the entering freshmen drop out before their junior year. Many professors still are teaching in the tradition of the manufacturing era, which was not any good then, and is obviously poor, at best, for the information era. But professors do not have time to experiment with new teaching techniques, to innovate, to try and fail/succeed because of the administrative emphasis on short-term results.

Disease 3: Evaluation of performance, merit rating, or annual review.

Performance reviews of faculty at most institutions are poorly done and are not statistically valid. Almost no performance reviews of faculty are associated with professional development opportunities and therefore act as mechanisms to build in fear and competition rather than cooperation. Probably the most devastating thing about faculty performance reviews is that they encourage faculty members to do what has been done in the past and accepted by the academy, rather than to experiment with new, controversial teaching/learning styles that may be considered immediate failures, but which may be highly successful for future generations.

Performance reviews of administrators work similarly. Imagine a mediocre vice president for academic affairs (VPAA) trying to impress his or her president about how well she or he performed during the past year. The VPAA, in order to make himself or herself look better, ranks the deans poorly so that in the eyes of the president she or he does not look as bad as was anticipated. Similarly, deans often evaluate faculty with the same results. Such an approach encourages tradition and conformity and inhibits creative approaches to teaching.

Often, faculty evaluate students without considering learning styles and teaching techniques which accommodate them, preferring to rely on "objective" standards.

Since merit pay is usually tied to an annual performance evaluations, we believe it is an inexpensive way to destroy the morale of an entire institution, as well as to discourage cooperation and innovation.

One of the greatest breakthroughs in higher education will occur when some institution develops a non-threatening, statistically significant, constructive performance review that encourages professional development, innovation, and quality.

Disease 4: Mobility of top management

It is not hard to imagine why there is such a large turnover in the administrative ranks in the colleges and universities in the United States. Take, for example, a dean who arrives at an institution intending to institute new and exciting ideas on teaching, research, and community service. Soon, however, s/he discovers that the faculty and staff are attempting only to survive the semester and are doing their best to impress the dean so that they may receive positive annual performance evaluations. Other demands creep into the daily routine. However, like most administrators coming with a fresh perspective and from another institution, s/he knows of ways to circumvent the archaic traditions. After a two-year window, the faculty, staff, administrators, and union representatives begin to adapt to the dean's new routines and find ways to impede further progress so that the dean must conform in order to survive.

The demands on the presidents' time are tremendous: fund-raising, alumni affairs, concerns of the board members, and issues raised by legislators. As a result, they are usually unable to devote much time to assist deans. The same holds true for vice presidents, who are concerned with acquiring the resources to operate their respective units, evaluating personnel, and finding ways to maintain the status quo. As a result they are usually too busy to assist deans.

Deans do what is necessary to survive in the outmoded system. Since there is no top-down drive to improve quality, to look at the long-term picture, to innovate, to develop collegiality, to involve everyone in planning and development, deans, who have seen a modicum of change during the first three or four years, begin to search for other opportunities to experience a two year adrenalin rush toward the elusive goal of pride in workmanship. (It is interesting to note that the creative activities and research endeavors expected of administrators are probably much less than what is expected of the faculty, yet the administration controls the processes and systems and theoretically could make time for these activities.)

When academic institutions have a firm commitment for establishing TQI from the governing board, president, vice presidents, deans, and chairpersons, they will not only retain good administrators, but there will be a rush of both administrators and faculty applying for positions.

Disease 5: Running an institution on visible figures alone

For most colleges and universities, the number of students is directly related to the institution's bragging rights. Some of the more prestigious institutions brag about the high number of quality applicants they had to reject. Resources are allocated to institutions based on the number of students and other factors such as the size of the physical facility. Entire budgets are allocated to academic departments based on the number of student credit hours generated. In the aforementioned examples, the quality of the educational experience is usually not even considered.

If quality and innovation were primary factors in planning, they would be reflected in resource allocation.

We have not exhausted the examples of the deadly diseases and obstacles confronting colleges and universities. We believe, however, if a college or university introduces a system for the transformation toward quality and innovation, it will become an infectious culture resulting in an immunity against mediocrity.

In summary, the Deming philosophy is to reduce variability in work processes by using statistical tools, and to establish a management style that is supportive of ongoing improvement. Deming believes that the **main reason for working is to have fun.** As we will elaborate upon later, before one can have fun at the work place, quality must be part of the institutional culture.

Deming believes that quality is never a problem, but a solution to problems. He and Juran (see below) support the concept that managers control 85 percent of the work system and workers control 15 percent. Since people work in the system, the main job of management is to improve the system with the help of workers. Deming believes that quality management is the ability to treat the problems of systems and the problems of people simultaneously.

Deming, as well as the other gurus of quality, believes successful organizations are customer-driven, and he supports the concept that everyone is a customer and must receive the respect and service commensurate with that title.

The Juran Approach

Joseph Juran (1988) believes management must establish top-level plans for annual improvement, and encourages projects as a means to achieve the improvement. The Juran philosophy seems to appeal to boss-type managers, since it makes them feel more in "control."

Juran's philosophy indicates that poor planning by management results in poor quality. His approach for improving quality is (1) to plan, (2) control, and (3) improve — known as the Juran trilogy. Let us review these techniques in greater detail.

- **Quality planning.** The process for preparing to meet institutional goals. According to Juran, the end result should be a process that is capable of meeting those goals under operating conditions. Quality planning might include identifying internal and external customers; determining customer needs; developing a product or service that responds to those needs; establishing goals that meet the needs of customers and suppliers at a minimum cost; and proving that the process is capable of meeting quality goals under operating conditions. To have quality planning in universities and colleges, managers must involve cross-functional teams and openly supply data to team members so they may work together to meet the needs of "customers," — in most cases, faculty and students.

- **Quality control.** A process for meeting goals under operating conditions, and requires collecting and analyzing data. One may have to decide on control subjects, units of measurement, standards of performance, and measurement of performance. To measure the difference between the actual performance before and after the process and/or system was modified, the data should be statistically significant and the processes and/or system should be in statistical control. The task forces working on various problems need to establish baseline data so they can determine if the implemented recommendations are causing an improvement.

- **Quality improvement.** The process for breaking through to a new level of performance. The end result is that the particular process and/or system is obviously at a higher level of quality in either delivering a product or service.

Juran's philosophy stresses the involvement of employees in task forces, much as does Waterman (1989). The philosophy and procedure require that managers listen to employees and help them rank the processes and systems that require improvement. This can be done through a nominal group ranking process as described in the next chapter. It is unlikely, however, that any unit — the president's office, the VPAA's office, the dean's office, or the academic department — can undertake more than two to three major projects per year for improvement. It is also obvious that management cannot delegate the reviewing of the recommended plan of action from the task force, or the actual resource allocation process to address the plan of action. Managers must also serve on the task forces, but rarely, if ever, as the chairperson. Managers must also provide recognition to the entire task force, not the chairperson alone, after the project is completed.

Figure 1.1 (next page) is an example of a plan, control, and improve approach using a **plan-do-check-act** (P-D-C-A) process, as previously described by Shewhart (Deming 1982, p. 88). In this example, the original zone of control displays a high level of poor quality, even if the system is stable. The "original zone of quality" became accepted as the cost of doing business. No one tried to improve the processes or the

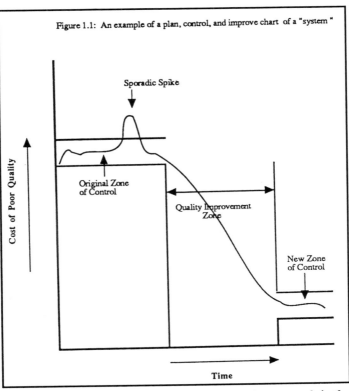

Figure 1.1: An example of a plan, control, and improve chart of a "system"

Sporadic Spike

Original Zone of Control

Quality Improvement Zone

New Zone of Control

Cost of Poor Quality

Time

system. The high **cost of quality** (COQ), although accepted, is the result of poor planning by management. However, as in most systems, a spike periodically occurs and the system is known to be out of control. When this happens, management is usually made aware of the problem(s) and a commitment is made to improve the process or system. Then management appoints a task force to study the problem and to make recommendations. When the recommendations are implemented, a zone of improvement usually occurs which eventually leads to a new zone of control, where the processes and system become stable and the cost of quality is reduced significantly. Juran, like Deming, Crosby, and Imai, believes that even this new zone of quality should be constantly addressed for additional improvement.

In manufacturing organizations, the cost of poor quality has been estimated to be between 25 to 30 percent of doing business. Juran and Crosby believe the "Cost of Poor Quality" in service organizations (colleges and universities?) is 40 percent of the total cost of doing business.

Many of the processes and systems in higher education can be adjusted and improved by using the Juran philosophy and the "plan-do-check-act" (P-D-C-A) approach. For example, the following case study reveals how one university used the P-D-C-A approach to improve the registration process.

Case Study: Student Registration

Student registration at one university was a constant disaster: there were never enough seats available for incoming freshmen even though the number of students could be statistically predicted with great accuracy. Every semester the quick-fix "cure" of increasing class sizes had to be initiated in every section of general education courses. Students were crammed into classrooms. Professors, instead of conducting classes for 35 students, in which some discussion and proper quality assessments could be undertaken, had to lecture to classes of 50 or more, where little or no discussion could be conducted. Tests typically consisted of multiple choice, fill in the blank, and true/false questions. Less importance was placed on quality educational experiences as quantity became more important. Obviously, barriers were not removed from either the professors' or the students' right to pride in workmanship, but were thrust in the way of the professor's ability to provide a quality education.

The vice president of academic affairs appointed a task force to exam the problem and make recommendations. They used the P-D-C-A technique and discovered that:

1. The number of seats assigned to general education courses were determined by the class scheduling process.
2. Class schedules were based upon the data received from the dean of institutional research and planning and the vice president of recruiting. The school deans and the chairpersons prepared the schedule.
3. Data provided to the school deans and chairpersons was accurate.
4. Based upon reasonable funding formulae provided by other state systems, the institution should have sufficient dollars to handle the expected number of students.

When the seat availability issue was examined, problems with several related systems were exposed:

1. It took eight months to print the class schedule (and still six errata sheets had to be added to the schedule).

2. The faculty hiring system was extremely cumbersome and involved over 30 steps. (A small group of managers impacted the faculty hiring process by making decisions based on stress points rather than on trust and statistically driven data.)

3. The faculty, chairpersons, and school deans failed to examine course requirements for majors and conducted business as usual.

As a result of the task force's recommendations, the class schedule printing system and the faculty hiring system were assigned to other task forces and are presented as case studies later in this text. Implementing the recommendations for the course scheduling system and its processes resulted in a dramatic and significant improvement for producing better schedules.

Let us examine the last system briefly:

As mentioned previously, the task force determined that the recruiting office and the office of the dean of institutional research and planning gave accurate information to chairpersons and school deans as to the anticipated size of the incoming class, both freshmen and transfers. The data also accurately reflected the number of majors by academic department. At this time they discovered that the chairpersons and dean had been preparing class schedules based not only on previous history but also the projected data for the incoming classes. They found that even during periods of declining enrollments in many disciplines, many departments continued to routinely schedule the same number of classes.

Many disciplines had so few majors that many of the upper division courses could have either been scheduled every second or third year or eliminated. Several programs had such a high faculty-to-student ratio that, for the cost per major, the students could have been given complete scholarships to private research universities — and it still would have saved money for taxpayers! By eliminating certain upper-division courses that contributed little to the major, and by eliminating some very low-enrollment programs that were outdated, demonstrated little potential for growth or need for the service region, and which did not service the general education requirements of this university, the need for approximately 15 FTE faculty positions was eliminated. All of these positions were taken either from projected overload and/or from the projected requirement for new faculty. At $50,000 per year per faculty member (salary plus benefits), the institution saved $750,000 annually simply by improving scheduling processes.

The Crosby Approach

Philip B. Crosby's philosophy seems to appeal to the human resource type of manager. Crosby enforces the belief that quality is a universal goal and that management must provide the leadership to compel an enterprise in which quality is never compromised.

Crosby defines quality as conformance to requirements. He believes the system of quality is prevention — that is appraisal is done now, not later. He encourages a performance standard of zero defects (ZD) and says that the measurement of quality is the price of non-conformance — doing something over rather than doing it right the first time. He believes managers should be facilitators and should be considered as such by employees, rather than as punishment sent from God.

Like Deming, Philip B. Crosby (1984, p. 99) has 14 steps for quality improvement. They are:

1.   *Management commitment.*
2.   *Quality improvement team.*
3.   *Measurement.*
4.   *Cost of quality.*
5.   *Quality awareness.*
6.   *Corrective action.*
7.   *ZD planning.*
8.   *Employee education.*
9.   *ZD Day.*
10.   *Goal setting.*
11.   *Error-cause removal.*
12.   *Recognition.*
13.   *Quality councils.*
14.   *Do it over again.*

Let us briefly examine each of the points and consider how they might be applied to institutions of higher education.

Point 1: Management Commitment

Crosby, like all of the quality gurus, makes the point that before lasting change toward quality can be realized, management must be trained in quality processes and systems, and must make it clear that they will support the commitment toward quality. At Philip Crosby

Associates, the following quality commitment directs every employees' job performance:

> *We will perform defect-free work for our clients and our associates. We will fully understand the requirements for our jobs and the systems that support us. We will conform to those requirements at all times* (Crosby 1984, p. 103).

How many presidents would make a similar statement about their college or university? How many presidents, vice presidents, and deans in institutions of higher education are even knowledgeable about quality processes and systems? If colleges and universities are serious about quality education, they should not only spell out the competencies of their graduates, but they should also guarantee the employers of their graduates that, if the graduates are found to be defective in the specified announced terminal competencies, the institution will "rework" the defective graduate for free!

Point 2: Quality Improvement Team

To get the entire organization to adopt the new quality philosophy — which is Deming's second point as well — Crosby (1984, p. 106) states that quality improvement teams should be formed. The team should consist of individuals who represent all the organization's functions. The team's primary function is to set up educational activities for all units.

Cross-functional teams are rare in higher education: it is uncommon to place secretaries, custodial personnel, human relations personnel, building and grounds personnel, police, faculty, management, union officers, and students on a team to do anything. One can only speculate what would happen if such a team were established to implement a TQI culture on campus.

Case Study: Involve Everyone Except the Faculty

At the time of a vacancy for the vice president for academic affairs (VPAA) position, the president insisted that all sectors of the campus be represented on the search committee. When one dean mentioned that it seemed inappropriate to search for the VPAA without having faculty represented on the committee, the remark was treated with amusement. The president later appointed a search committee of some eight individuals, including the head of the campus police force, a former secretary he had just elevated to assistant to the president, and the head of the local chapter of the maintenance union.

The person that was selected had no prior administrative experience. In fact, this person did not ever possess tenure at a college or university, and had only very limited teaching experience at the grade school level. The committee had overlooked several highly qualified and experienced individuals who had both extensive faculty and administrative experience.

Candidates for any position certainly put forth an enormous amount of time and effort into applying, but even more so for top-level management positions. An analysis of the cost involved in search committees would be revealing, particularly at institutions where in a short time period the same position is re-advertised.

Obviously, the formation of cross-functional teams should involve people who will be directly affected by the outcome of the task. The extreme disparities between functions in the previous example is uncommon, but that such a thing could occur is unconscionable. Still, too frequently presidents, having hand-picked a selection committee, fail to have the final candidates interview with the staff that they will directly manage.

Point 3: Measurement

Crosby makes the point of establishing baseline data to evaluate the improvement process. He states that people become frustrated when such data is not available and, as a result, they don't have an indication as to how they are doing.

In Chapter 3 we suggested an evaluation and scoring procedure for obtaining a **quality index** (QI) for institutions of higher education. The benefit of the QI tool is that it can help to establish a baseline for the institution and each unit and/or department within the institution.

If faculty, staff, and students do not know how they are progressing toward the announced quality goals, they will become frustrated and will operate under their own rules, insisting that their actions are resulting in a quality output.

Point 4: The Cost of Quality

Crosby (1984, p. 110) recommends that a special workshop for the organization's comptroller and other interested individuals be conducted so they can establish a procedure for their accounting system. He recommends that the cost accounting procedure be pulled together in an orderly fashion so all that is described is measured in the same manner all the time.

It is not unusual for colleges and universities within the same state system to measure head count, cost per student credit hour, cost per FTE student, cost per major, etc. in entirely different ways. In fact, meaningful comparison between institutions sometimes becomes nearly impossible. Moreover, it is not unusual within one institution for data between departments to be entered and interpreted in different ways, so that meaningful baseline data is almost impossible to establish.

Point 5: Quality Awareness

Crosby states (1984, p. 111) that quality has to become part of the corporate culture. Everyone should understand that management is committed to quality, and therefore quality is the policy. He emphasizes that the employees must be informed on the cost of not doing a task correctly the first time.

In making employees aware of the cost of nonconformance, Crosby gives an example of a company that borrowed 10 new Cadillac automobiles, parked them on the front lawn and informed employees that those automobiles represented the cost of troubleshooting. However, what are the real costs to society when institutions of higher education fail to graduate competent students?

Somewhere between one-third to one-half of a dean's time is used to check on forms and data already submitted and checked by another employee! Deans become mired with insignificant details, which detracts from the time spent with faculty in moving the academy forward. If, on the other hand, TQM and TQI were adopted, more time could be spent on collaborative projects to improve the quality of education.

Point 6: Corrective Action

The main purpose of corrective action, according to Crosby, is to identify problems and take actions necessary to eliminate them. Corrective action is **not** redoing someone else's mistakes. Corrective action procedures should be based on data and can only be effective if the system under investigation is in statistical control. Corrective action steps may involve identifying suppliers who are not meeting conformance standards and then communicating precisely what you expect from their product or service.

Corrective action steps require the empowerment of employees to bring to the administration's attention things that are not only done incorrectly, but also what could be done better and more efficiently.

41

Corrective action requires teamwork coupled through quality circles and action-oriented task forces. Corrective action is a major part of the P-D-C-A cycle mentioned previously and is an essential part of TQI and TQM.

Point 7: Zero Defects Planning

Planning for a zero defects (ZD) day, according to Crosby (1984, p. 114), could take considerable time. It might represent more than a year or so after the quality process is instituted. In planning for the zero defect day, he suggests that representatives from major suppliers and customers, as well as from unions and people outside the company, be included. In academic institutions we recommend not only faculty, staff, and administration be represented, but also students from major student-based organizations, as well as their parents and representatives from the city or region.

Point 8: Employee Education

After management is educated about TQI and TQM, train all employees in such philosophy and procedures. Crosby's method requires 30 hours of classroom instruction with additional time for homework (1984, p. 115). (Using the method described in Chapter 4, we noticed that approximately 35 hours of training was required in addition to 90 hours for homework assignments.)

When faculty and staff understand the principles and procedures of TQI, they will develop greater pride in their work. We also believe that if faculty use TQI procedures and apply them in the classroom, students will take an active part in their own education.

Point 9: Zero Defects Day

Zero defects day is that day when top managers stand up in front of everyone and announce they are committed to quality. Crosby (1984, p. 116) suggests that the zero defects day should be well-planned and dignified.

Announcing a ZD day for an institution of higher education would be a major undertaking, since it would require that every employee and student become responsible for quality experiences, products and services.

Point 10: Goal Setting

Goal setting, according to Crosby (1984, p. 116), is something that happens when the organization begins to gather data to measure improvements. Of course, data is needed by any institution, colleges and universities included, to establish a baseline of performance.

We recommend that every department post charts and graphs displaying baseline data, as well as projected goals, in every department. For example, historical data of student retention rates may demonstrate that a certain department has an attrition rate of 15 percent. After better advising, testing, mentoring, and tutoring procedures are implemented, the department may experience a decrease in the attrition rate over the following three years.

Point 11: Error-Cause Removal

Crosby (1984, p. 117) states that error-cause removal is having employees point out what is wrong with the processes and systems, but not necessarily how they might be improved.

We recommend that departments within academic institutions use the nominal group process for ranking the top two or three major problems that require the attention of either unit managers or top management. We have found the Ishikawa diagram ("fishbone charts") to be effective in identifying many causes of major problems. The Ishikawa diagrams and a procedure for a nominal group process are described in Chapter 2. By seriously considering the input of all employees, using these techniques we have found a greater sense of teaming among employees.

Point 12: Recognition

Both Crosby (1984, p. 119) and Deming believe merit pay is a very bad form of recognition. Crosby, however, believes that a serious recognition program for good employees should be created, since it is a very important part of the quality movement. Crosby does his recognition awards at an annual black-tie picnic.

We believe merit pay in institutions of higher education is an inexpensive way of getting everyone in the organization mad at each other. On the other hand, we believe that recognizing **individuals** and **groups** for efforts in establishing and/or improving quality should be done annually. In one school, quality awards are granted in the following order of **increasing importance:**

1. Best researcher.
2. Best provider of community service.
3. Best innovator.
4. Best teacher.
5. Best academic department.

Whereas nominations for the best researcher, service provider, innovator, and teacher are requested from the faculty, the school dean makes the final selection. The best academic department is determined by a modified Malcolm Baldrige Award procedure as described in Chapter 3. Every member of the department is awarded a "Quality" pin (as are individual winners). The department award is an eloquent, display-worthy placard or sculpture, and the awards ceremony occurs at the school's annual retreat. We recommend that each institution of higher education establish such recognition ceremonies and that the ceremonies be presided over by high-ranking managers, preferably the president of the institution.

Point 13: Quality Councils

Crosby (1984, p. 119) states *the idea of quality councils is to bring the quality professionals together and let them learn from each other. This is an excellent way to keep the organization focused on 'quality' issues and to prevent slippage to traditional manners of operation.* Whereas Deming encourages total involvement of the customer and the supplier, Crosby's point on instituting "quality councils" is truly necessary to ensure the constant and tedious reminders needed to keep the institution pointed in the same direction.

"Quality councils" are necessary for educational institutions, since too many presidents, managers, and faculty believe TQI and TQM programs are not applicable to educational institutions.

Point 14: Do it Over Again

All of the quality gurus agree that improvement is constant and never complete. Crosby (1984, pp. 119-120), however, makes several remarks regarding this point that should be fully comprehended:

Education has to be a vital part of the relationship. The difference between manufacturing and service is whether the product finally does something for the customer or an individual does.

Like Deming's five sins, Crosby (1984, pp. 2-5) has his own five "sins" for troubled organizations. They are:

1. *The outgoing product or service normally contains deviations from published, announced, or agreed-upon requirements.*

2. *The company has an extensive field service or dealer network skilled in rework and resourceful corrective action to keep customers satisfied.*

3. *Management does not provide a clear performance standard or definition of quality, so each employee develops his/her own.*

4. *Management does not know the price of non-conformance.*

5. *Management denies responsibility for problems.*

We will examine these "sins" in greater detail, since they apply to both manufacturing organizations and institutions of higher education.

1.   The outgoing product or service normally contains deviations from published, announced, or agreed-upon requirements.

Crosby mentions that service companies do not document their quality (nonconformances) with the rigor of product-producing companies.

Institutions of higher education, especially comprehensive colleges and universities, often claim that their graduates are liberally educated and able to speak, read, write, and analyze critically. The truth of the matter is that far too many college graduates do not speak, read and write well enough to satisfy employers and others who expect college-level communication skills.

2.   The company has an extensive field service or dealer network skilled in rework, and resourceful corrective action to keep customers satisfied.

In institutions of higher education, corrective action is taken through divisions of continuing education, re-training and re-educating employees who were inadequately prepared the first time around. Of course, divisions of continuing education serve as a valuable service and are needed as many professions require updating to remain current. This is especially essential for the science-based professions. Still, like many companies, whose field service contracts represent a large proportion of their revenues, divisions of continuing education at "better" ranked institutions continue to generate profits in the millions of dollars doing what should have been done by many institutions during the undergraduate education experience.

In every institution of higher education we have been associated with over the past 35 years, we know of redundant processes and systems where individuals are assigned functions of checking and re-doing work that should have been done right in the first place. Like many companies who have individuals doing nothing but rework, institutions of higher education have people assigned to check, check and re-check something as simple as generating a catalog or schedule of courses. This is in addition to faculty teaching in the divisions of continuing education — usually making an additional salary.

3.   **Management does not provide a clear performance standard or definition of quality, so each employee develops his/her own.**

Like companies with poor management, many institutions of higher education permit employees to create their own performance standards — and the public continues to support this endeavor. For example, at many public institutions one-half of the students who enter never graduate. There are two main reasons for the high dropout rate: (1) students were permitted entrance into the institution who were not educationally prepared for college; and (2) the professors cannot teach effectively — if we consider motivation to be an essential part of TQI and TQM.

By defining clear performance standards we mean that every institution should convey honest position descriptions when advertising for faculty. Often the position descriptions in the classifieds of professional journals imply that jobs will provide ample opportunity to do research, when in fact, the actual jobs require: (1) teaching large, multiple sections of general-education courses for non-majors, (2) teaching one upper-division course for majors, (3) advising 40 students per year, and (4) serving on four institutional committees.

The question of emphasis should be addressed by institutions prior to placement of advertisements and prior to any selection process. Institutions should be clear about what they are seeking and clear in wording advertisements so experience and credentials are not left up to interpretation by potential applicants or members of the search committee. A great deal of unnecessary applications could be avoided if clarity could be achieved, and a good deal of unnecessary time could be saved if screening committees did not demand reference letters and transcripts until a secondary phase in the selection process.

Finalists for positions usually spend between one and two days on

46

campus for the actual interview. In many cases prior telephone interviews help narrow the field, and in a few extraordinary cases visits to the applicant's home campus are made for the same purpose. A lot of what is done has to do with the availability of budget to complete the task, but money need not and should not determine whether the institution has conducted its work properly.

Usually four or five finalists are invited to campus for often toilsome meetings with various constituencies. Turnout at open meetings usually depends on the time of day they are scheduled, and of course, if the school is not in session, the turnout is likely to be slight. From an institutional viewpoint, the candidates are being tested for how they will perform when confronted with the very people with whom they will come in contact. Prepared questions are asked of each candidate, often with calculated precision to the detriment of a real exchange of views and opinions.

Successful candidates usually are good speakers, because that is the real focus for the interview process. There is usually no opportunity to observe how the candidate writes — that is usually taken wrongly as a given — or how the candidate works with individuals or groups. The "public" speaking forum of the process is the key determinant. Search committees members have been known to discount what a candidate says in favor of how the candidate fared at the lunch or dinner occasion.

Few institutions require a great deal of public speaking or formal dinner occasions with the constituencies under the individual. While these certainly occur, the real focus for the individual's job is related more to one-on-one meetings, decision making, telephone contacts, and interaction among peers at administrative meetings. In typical interview processes these situations are not simulated so no advance reading of the candidates can be gained.

We are aware of one university that required job-related simulations. A dean or vice president, for example, would be asked to outline a strategy for implementation relating to a real or imaginary situation facing the institution. The responses would be carefully analyzed by the search committee for validity and feasibility. The results are quite revealing. Several finalists seemed befuddled by situations they would undoubtedly face; others revealed by the outlines that they would omit necessary steps, explanations, or concepts; and others demonstrated that they understood what was involved and offered reasonable, logical approaches to solving the problems. Those who understand the approaches and principles of TQM and TQI do well in such interviews.

47

4.   Management does not know the price of non-conformance.

Whereas product companies spend 20 percent or more of their sale dollars doing things wrong and re-doing the work (Crosby 1984, p. 5), it is conservatively estimated that such activities cost service companies 40 percent. Since higher education is a service, why should public institutions of higher education be any different? We contend that these institutions could significantly reduce waste and redoing costs by adopting TQM and TQI.

5.   Management denies that it is the cause of the problem.

Crosby (1984, p. 5) states *most managers send everyone else to school, set up 'programs' for the lowest levels of the organization and make speeches with impressive sounding words... The main obstacle to improvement is the stubbornness of management.* Why is it that so few managers and union leaders in institutions of higher education refuse to believe that they may learn something about quality if they attended a Philip B. Crosby management school? Crosby makes a strong case for the professional development of managers so they are capable of understanding and implementing quality processes.

Case Study: Course Scheduling

Crosby emphasizes the point: **Do it right the first time!** The following case study was taken from a university which was having difficulty producing an error-free class schedule. In fact, it took up to eight months from the initial request of the academic dean to submit a class schedule to the actual publication of the schedule. To exacerbate matters, the final schedule contained many errors. Obviously, it was not done right the first time.

Figure 1.2 (next page) shows the various tasks performed to produce a class schedule:

1.   The academic dean wrote a memo to the associate dean of academic affairs requesting that he begin the process of producing a schedule.

2.   To not belabor the point we will mention the following involvement of personnel only once: the secretary had to type the memo, the academic dean had to sign the memo, the secretary had to mail it to the associate dean of academic affairs, and the mail room personnel had to deliver the mail. When the mail arrived to the office of the associate dean of academic affairs, the secretary had to open the mail, sort the mail, and bring the item

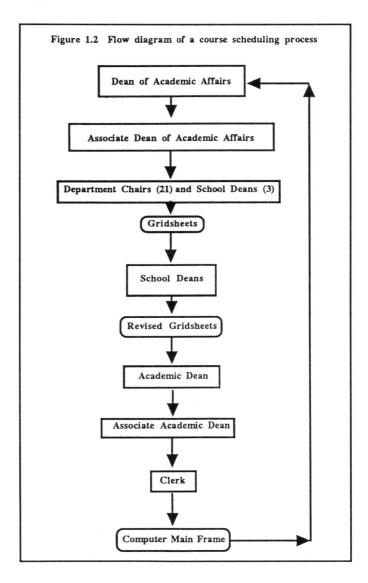

Figure 1.2 Flow diagram of a course scheduling process

Dean of Academic Affairs

Associate Dean of Academic Affairs

Department Chairs (21) and School Deans (3)

Gridsheets

School Deans

Revised Gridsheets

Academic Dean

Associate Academic Dean

Clerk

Computer Main Frame

to his attention. The same would be true for the offices of the 21 chairpersons and three school deans.

3.   The associate dean for academic affairs wrote a memo to the 21 department chairpersons with copies to the three school deans asking them to complete a "schedule-sheet." The schedule-sheet

was a spreadsheet that has entries for: the Department Name, Course Section, Course Number, Course Title, Days Scheduled, Time Scheduled, Credit Hours (CH) of the course, and the professor's name.

The **schedule-sheet** had several major drawbacks. First of all, it had to be completed by hand and under no circumstance would a typed or computer generated sheet be acceptable. Secondly, **credit hours** (CH) differed from faculty **load hours** (LH). Faculty were paid by load hours, and one could not receive the necessary information from the schedule-sheets about the projected faculty workload. Only CH's were entered and LH's did not necessarily correlate with CH's, especially in the case of laboratory courses or in courses that had combined lecture sections, but different clinical or discussion sections. The data entry problem was the result of **poor computer programming** from a unit not directly responsible for the preparation of courses — or so they thought. As will be demonstrated later, one of the major causes of the scheduling fiasco was the direct result of poor leadership in the department of computer services, a major supplier for the process.

4.   The department chairpersons submitted their recommended schedules to their school dean.

5.   The school deans, after consultation with the chairpersons, submitted the revised schedule-sheets (course schedules) to the academic dean.

6.   The academic dean forwarded the proposed schedules to the associate academic dean.

7.   The associate academic dean assigned a clerk to enter each course from the schedule-sheets into the computer main frame.

As mentioned above, the computer program could not differentiate between courses that had shared lecture sections and separate laboratory sections, and as a result, the data indicated that some faculty were greatly overloaded, while others were teaching at a significant underload. The members of the department of computer services denied that they were part of the problem!

8.   The final schedule, including all of the errors entered by the parties involved and those in the computer program, required at least **three** additional cycles of the first eight steps to produce a schedule that required no more than **six** errata sheets after being published!

A task force looked into the problem and recommended an obvious solution that utilized the campus' electronic mail technology, a process

50

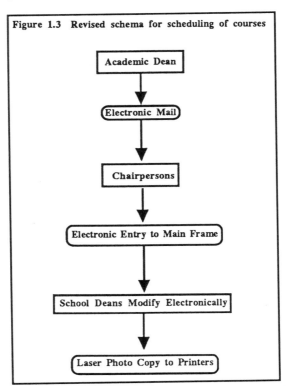

Figure 1.3   Revised schema for scheduling of courses

Academic Dean

Electronic Mail

Chairpersons

Electronic Entry to Main Frame

School Deans Modify Electronically

Laser Photo Copy to Printers

that empowered the chairpersons and the dean to enter error-free schedules directly onto the main frame. What previously took eight months to accomplish, now took five working days! The recommended process is shown in Figure 1.3 (above).

This case study demonstrates how Crosby's TQM quality philosophy could greatly improve the efficiency of institutions of higher education.

The Imai Approach

Imai (1986) supports the continuous improvement process where people are encouraged to focus on the processes and systems in which they work, rather than on the results. He believes that by continually improving the processes and systems, the end result will be a better product or service. This has become known as the "P" or process approach, rather than the "R" or results approach of Frederick Taylor (1911). The process approach is also known as the Kaizen approach.

Figure 1.4 (next page) depicts the differences between the "R" and the "P" approaches. In the "R" approach, management examines the

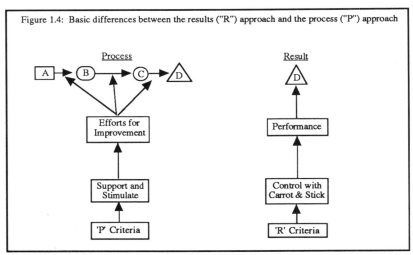

Figure 1.4: Basic differences between the results ("R") approach and the process ("P") approach

anticipated result(s), usually pre-determined by Management by Objectives, then rates the performance of the individual(s). The person's performance is influenced by reward and punishment: that is, the use of "carrot and stick" motivation. In the "P" approach, management supports the individual's and team's efforts to improve the processes and systems leading to the end result.

The continuous improvement, or Kaizen approach, has a long-term, undramatic affect on a process or system. Change is gradual and consistent. The approach involves everyone and the resulting group effort is focused on processes and systems rather than one person's performance evaluation. The approach has low monetary investment on the part of management, but requires a great deal of effort by management to maintain the group process. The Kaizen approach is people-oriented.

The typical approach used by many institutions of higher education is totally different. Most colleges and universities seek a quick, dramatic fix to their problems. The technical approach used by many of institutions demand a short-term, but dramatic approach ("up the seat counts" because they did not plan) that results in abrupt and volatile changes. The technical approach in most institutions usually involves a select few, and individual results are measured and evaluated rather than the results from teamwork.

Figure 1.5 (next page) shows the interactions between five interrelated systems, namely, the **recruiting office data, institutional research and planning data, course scheduling, class schedule production and student registration.** What began as a study to

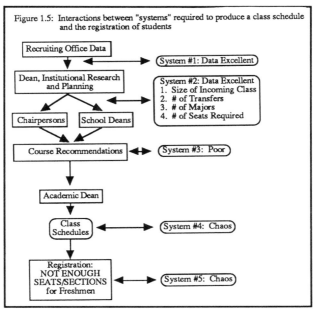

Figure 1.5: Interactions between "systems" required to produce a class schedule and the registration of students

determine why there was not a sufficient number of seats and sections of general education courses for incoming freshmen, pointed to major problems in the related systems of course scheduling and faculty hiring. The study also predicted a potentially major problem in not having enough upper-division courses and seats. Such are the benefits of the Imai approach!

In summary, this chapter reviewed briefly the total quality improvement (TQI) and total quality management (TQM) philosophies of Deming, Juran, Crosby, and Imai, and how they might be applied to institutions of higher education. Several case studies of poor processes and systems at universities were given. Each of the quality leaders stresses the importance of clear performance standards, support and training for meeting them, organization-wide commitment to quality, and the participation of all employees in TQM and TQI.

Chapter 2:
Principles of Total Quality Management

In Chapter 1, we identified and clarified the total quality management (TQM) and total quality improvement (TQI) models of Deming, Juran, Crosby, and Imai. Although different in some respects, they each have common elements. The purpose of this chapter is to examine the common elements of the quality experts and suggest how they may be applied to institutions of higher education.

The seven common elements that bind the foundations of TQM and TQI by Deming, Juran, Crosby, and Imai are:

1. Processes and systems.

2. Teaming.

3. Customers and suppliers.

4. Quality by fact, process, and perception.

5. Management by fact.

6. Complexity.

7. Variation.

Let us examine each of these common elements.

Processes and Systems

All of the combined tasks or steps necessary to accomplish a given result is defined as a process. A series of related processes is called a system. Whereas people have a natural tendency to describe their work in terms of "results," such as "I am a teacher," the result is the end product of a series of tasks or steps.

Even though Imai can be considered the champion in using the **process** ("P") approach over the more commonly used **result** ("R") approach, the other leaders in quality also stress the importance of improving processes and systems in which employees work to constantly improve the quality of goods and services. Deming, Juran, and Crosby stress that since management controls at least 85 percent of the processes and systems in which employees work, most of the blame for poor quality rests with poor management and a strict emphasis on results, not processes.

If it's assumed that every work activity is a part of a process and system, there are countless processes and systems that exist in every institution of higher education. If we assume that everyone wants to do a good job and that our institutions work through processes and systems, it follows that our institutions can improve only if we improve the processes and systems in which the employees work. If the managers of our academic institutions improve processes and systems, they will not only get better quality results, but better productivity as well. The same holds true for administrators and teachers in K-12 schools.

A "system" as used in this text is an arrangement of persons, places, things, and/or circumstances that either makes, facilitates, or permits things to happen. The very nature of a system will determine what will happen and how it will happen. We wish to make several points about the importance of understanding systems: By knowing a system it's possible to prevent errors by not permitting the system to try to handle something it was not designed to handle. By knowing the end product or service function one is trying to produce or accomplish, one should be able to design and choose a system to produce the product or perform the function. Still, a system which is effective for performing one task may not be appropriate for another. Although one should be able to predict the outcomes and behavior within a system, and thus alter either the outcomes or behavior, it is not always possible to infer the system's overall performance by examining its individual parts. Finally, it is possible that each of the different units within a university or college might very well have efficient systems, but the systems between the units may be incompatible.

Most administrators inherit organizations established by previous managers, and face the challenge of maintaining the strengths and eliminating the weaknesses of systems established by their predecessors.

Most likely they have entered situations governed by closed systems where anticipated results yield predictable attitudes and behaviors. This cycle of predictability is difficult to alter and inhibits change processes leading to quality. This is illustrated in Figure 2.1 (next page).

Since we assume that administrators control 85 to 90 percent of the processes and systems, we are convinced that if they seriously commit to quality, they can influence faculty and students to do likewise. Faculty and students will most likely work hard if they are convinced that quality will be the end result (Glasser 1990, p. 433). In fact, we agree with Dr. Glasser's comment that *quality is contagious* (p. 435). If management directs its energies toward improving processes and systems for quality results, with, of course, professors and staff responsible for providing and receiving the service, quality results will result in modified behavior, a better attitude and eventually an organizational culture directed toward

56

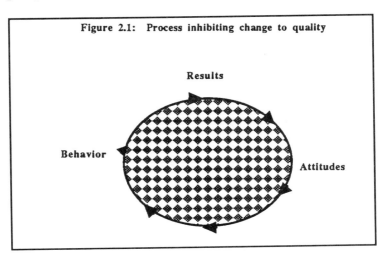

Figure 2.1: Process inhibiting change to quality

Results

Behavior

Attitudes

achieving quality. An example of this process is displayed in Figure 2.2.

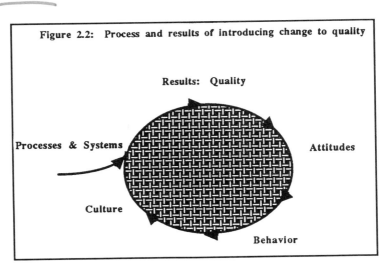

Figure 2.2: Process and results of introducing change to quality

Results: Quality

Processes & Systems

Attitudes

Culture

Behavior

Teaming

Teams and teamwork are extremely important for producing a quality service or product. Although hierarchy is needed within all organizations to prevent chaos, most work in institutions of higher education and other service organizations is accomplished across, not within, organizational boundaries. This cross-functional process model is shown in Figure 2.3 (next page).

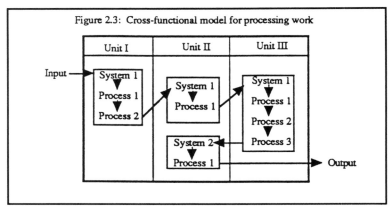

Figure 2.3: Cross-functional model for processing work

According to Hrebiniak (1978, p. 137)

... in organizations with strong hierarchial and status differences, communications will be vertical in nature, and often biased. Top-level personnel make important decisions and lower-level personnel implement them. This results in a predominantly up-down flow of task-related information. The respect for people of higher status may result in a reluctance to criticize their ideas, and cause the transmission of information that subordinates feel superiors would like to hear. The emphasis on vertical communications further suggests that the tall pyramidal organization performs best when tasks are not complex and most activity involves simple coordination... However, when problems are complex, individuals may be overwhelmed by the quantity of information... Thus, for non-routine, complex matters, the prognosis for effective problem solving in the hierarchial system does not appear to be a good one.

The informal power structure and the resulting culture in institutions of higher education do not readily permit collegiality in a management system based upon hierarchy. But teaming, when done properly, is invariably found in institutions having high morale.

In their recent books Waterman (1990) and Levering (1988) stress the importance of teamwork in effecting change and in keeping morale high.

Waterman says that a well-run project team can *cut across conventional lines and boundaries* and is *designed to effect change* (p. 6). He states that a well-run project team solves the problem of lousy implementation, one of management's most common problems. He does not, however, believe that bureaucracy should be destroyed, but that it must coexist with adhocracy (any organizational form that promotes collegial rather than bureaucratic behavior).

Levering states that being part of a team represents a risk, but *people cannot thrive unless they have some say in how much they wish to contribute (p. 217)*. He also stresses that all employees should have the right to full and accurate data, the right to free and open speech without the fear of reprisal, and a stake in the results, if trust, pride, and quality are to be the end results of teaming.

Managers and employees can achieve these results through training in Total Quality Improvement. Armed with the knowledge and skills of TQI, they should identify two or three processes which, in their organization, are responsible for poor quality products or services. These processes should be clearly and visibly targeted for improvement.

In fact, selecting processes that, if improved, will greatly advance either the quality of service provided or product produced, is one of the best and most highly recommended ways to approach changes toward an institutional culture of TQI and TQM. Waterman (1990), in his powerful book *Adhocracy: The Power to Change*, refers to means for getting people actively involved in embracing and effecting change. He suggests that people, under the proper leadership, will participate in meaningful task forces with the intention of changing their organization from one of non-quality to one of high quality.

An excellent way of helping people to embrace change is to identify the causes of poor quality through a nominal group process. For those not familiar with such a process, we describe one below. When this technique is used it soon becomes obvious that 80 percent of the problems are caused by a relatively few poor processes and systems. It is essential that employees be involved in identifying and ranking the importance of the problems if they are to be part of the cross-functional team for recommending solutions.

Nominal Group Process

Recognition of perceived problems and/or weaknesses inhibiting quality:

It is recommended that each group consist of five to 10 people and have a facilitator that is not part of the institutional planning process. Each facilitator will require a stopwatch during the workshop. Since large units will have several groups, it is possible, although unlikely, that each group may perceive different problems/weaknesses. If this should happen, it may be necessary to repeat the technique described herein for the entire unit before the final ranking can be assigned. The initial group selection within units should be assigned by the facilitator and should be made according to the diversity of individual backgrounds.

- **1. Procedure**

  ### a) Introduction to the process (5 minutes)

  The role of the facilitator: The facilitator is to provide instructions regarding the process but is not to influence the group's decision. The facilitator is to keep the group working within time limits.

  The Nominal Group Process: The nominal group process allows participants to explore areas systematically and to arrive at a consensus. The process consists of developing a list and ranking perceived problems. The results of the ranking are discussed, and the perceived problems which are the most important to the group are identified.

  ### b) Presentation of the question (15 minutes)

  The question to be considered: The facilitator should ask the group, "What is the major problem of your unit that affects quality?"

  Completion of Form A: The facilitator should repeat the question and ask each participant to take five minutes and write specific three- to five-word answers for each perceived problem on Form A, working silently and independently. After that time, if it appears that several members have not finished, the facilitator should state that s/he will allow two additional minutes. If most members have already finished, the facilitator will not allow the extra time.

  ### c) Development of a master list (20 minutes)

  Recitation and recording of perceived problems: While the group is developing their list of perceived problems, the facilitator should use an overhead and project Chart 1 (next page).

  At the end of the time allotted for listing the perceived problems of the unit, the facilitator should ask the participants to stop writing. Then in a round-robin fashion, the facilitator will ask each to read aloud one of her/his perceived problems on the list. The facilitator will tell the participants that if they come to a problem on their list that has been given, they need not repeat it. If one item is phrased differently from another but appears to be the same, the facilitator will ask the group members to indicate by a show of hands if they think the items are the same. If most of the group feel the items are the same, the perceived problem will not be listed again; otherwise, both items will be listed. It may be necessary during this time for the facilitator to ask the participants not to speak out of turn. There should be **no discussion** of the list at this point. As each perceived problem is given, the facilitator will record the item on the chart. The facilitator must **not** suggest categories or combinations. The items should be numbered and recorded as presented by the participants without editing, unless the item is too long, in which case the facilitator may try to shorten the phrasing of the perceived problem without changing the meaning. If at the end of 20 minutes some group members have items that have not been presented, the facilitator will ask each member to give the one **most important** perceived problem remaining on his list.

d) Master list item clarification (15 minutes)

The facilitator should point to each perceived problem on the master list and read the item aloud. The facilitator should ask if each item is understood. If an item is unclear, the facilitator should ask the individual

CHART 1

Facilitators Worksheet for Recording Perceived Problems that Inhibit Quality

Item Number	Perceived Problems	Initial Value	Final Value	Final Rank
1				
2				
3				
4				
5				
6				
7				
8				
9				

who generated the item to address and clarify it. The facilitator should **not** attempt to either condense the list nor to permit the group to discuss the relative importance of the perceived problems at this point. Remember, the purpose of this step is **clarification.**

request that each member select and rank the **five** most important perceived problems of the unit. The most important perceived problem should be assigned a number five; the next most important item should be assigned a number four; and so forth with the number one being assigned for the least important. The participants are to record their rankings on **Form B**, whereupon the facilitator should collect the forms and tally the results on the master list, giving each item an initial score.

f) Discussion of initial ranking (30 minutes)

The facilitator should discuss the rankings with participants, who may then wish to **elaborate, defend, and dispute** the rankings and combine categories. They may not add items. Items may be discussed even if they did not receive a high score. Groups should be reminded that this is their opportunity to express opinions and persuade others. The facilitator should attempt to keep the discussion orderly and prevent anyone from dominating.

g) Final listing and ranking of items (15 minutes)

After the items have been discussed the facilitator should distribute copy of **Form C** to all group members. The facilitator should request each member to rank the top five choices as before: assign number five to the item they consider the most important, and so on. At the end of the allocated time the facilitator should record the final values to each item on the master list.

The results of the master list should be recorded and typed on **Form D** as they might be discussed by the task force.

h) Break (20 minutes)

The facilitator should encourage participants to move about.

• **2. Forms to be completed**

Forms A through D are to be completed during the nominal group process. These are:

Form A: Listing perceived problems.

Form B: Initial ranking of perceived problems.

Form C: Final ranking of perceived problems.

Form D: Summary of the unit's perceived problems.

See the following pages for forms A-D.

FORM A

LISTING OF PERCEIVED PROBLEMS

Please respond to the following question with short but specific answers: WHAT DO YOU THINK ARE THE MAJOR PROBLEMS IN YOUR UNIT THAT INHIBITS QUALITY?

Item #	Perceived Problem
1	
2	
3	
4	
5	

Form B

Initial Ranking of Perceived Problems

Please refer to the master list that describes the perceived problems and indicate what you think are the five major problems

Item Number from The Master List	Initial Objective Ranking Value
	#5 (Most Important)
	#4
	#3
	#2
	#1 (Least Important)

Form C
Final Ranking of Perceived Problems
Please refer to the master list that describes the perceived problems and indicate what you think are the five major problems

Item Number from The Master List	Final Objective Ranking Value
	#5 (Most Important)
	#4
	#3
	#2
	#1 (Least Important)

Form D
Summary of Perveived Problems

This information is to be completed by the workshop facilitator and will be submitted to the quality task force for analysis and action

Item Number	Perceived Problem	Initial Value	Final Value	Final Rank
1				
2				
3				
4				
5				
6				
7				
8				
9				
10				
11				

Using the nominal group process, a college of arts and sciences identified the following problems/processes that inhibited quality. The comments that follow the ranked problems are from the facilitator's report.

Items Inhibiting Quality in the College of Arts and Sciences

1. Lack of facilities

The college did not have adequate facilities to serve the number of students or faculty. For example, the number of offices needed to house newly hired faculty would be inadequate. It was also noted that "inadequate facilities" would be a major national problem for all higher education and would eventually have to be addressed by the federal government. It was their feeling that this would remain the major perceived problem at the institution for quite some time.

2. Timeliness of administrative decisions

Many examples were given to demonstrate slow action on crucial requests. Foremost was the approval process for new faculty. Others included ordering equipment, supplies and computers; getting approval for alternate assignments; adding courses and sections; and getting budget transfer requests approved.

Much of what was discussed in other items could have easily been included in this point. As a result, this item would have been ranked first.

Timeliness of administrative decisions included discussions on:

1) Micro-management by administration.

2) Scheduling problems.

3) Cumbersome hiring processes.

4) Poor lateral communications outside of academic affairs.

3. Poor student profiles

The main examples included the poor quality of entering freshmen and the number of freshmen in relation to the total number of students, especially upper-division students.

In the past, the chairpersons had not suggested raising the entrance requirements. Now, however, they suggested a thorough assessment of incoming students with proper advising into remedial classes so eventual success could be more nearly assured. The chairs also suggested that a freshman year course be required for most students, and that a cooperative education program be implemented to increase the retention of students who had to work while attending the university. All of these excellent suggestions were considered by a task force, and were designed to increase retention and success rates, increase the upper-division population, and improve the quality of the student population, graduates, and eventually the school's reputation.

Some of these suggestions would be expensive to implement, whereas others could be accomplished at modest expense. All required a commitment for quality.

This college started a comprehensive "2+2" articulation agreement campaign with community colleges to increase the number of upper-division students in its majors.

4. Micro-management by administration

Much of what was mentioned in this point could be applied to point two: timeliness of decisions by administration. For example, one suggestion pertained to getting approval for the hiring of a faculty replacement. Some believed that this should be the responsibility of the provost/VPAA and should not require approval from an executive committee. Another dealt with the approval process for ordering computers: it was suggested that the computer center be removed from the approval process so requests could be processed more quickly and effectively. Some questioned the long delays of getting budget transfers approved by the VPAA office, especially on items agreed to by both the chairperson and dean. Some questioned the involvement of upper administration in the routine operations of the department, even to the point of requiring unnecessary, time-consuming responses by the chairperson.

Some of these problems could be quickly resolved through presidential approval; others require the application of situational management, an administrative philosophy inconsistent with the current institutional culture.

5. Uncommitted faculty

When the college had started its long-range planning process 18 months before, every department perceived the quality and commitment of its faculty to be a major strength. For the most part this was true; however, the perception of the "uncommitted faculty" as a major stumbling point to quality in the college came only after repeated nominal group processes. Initially, chairpersons were reluctant to discuss that perception, but as the nominal group process allows such issues to be raised, discussed and quantified, the problem of uncommitted faculty eventually received attention.

Once a problem has been identified and a project team established, the team must gather and analyze data from the processes and systems contributing to the perceived problem. After suggestions are recommended and implemented to rectify the problem, the processes and systems are standardized and evaluated, and plans for continuous improvement are implemented. This is illustrated in Figure 2.4 (below).

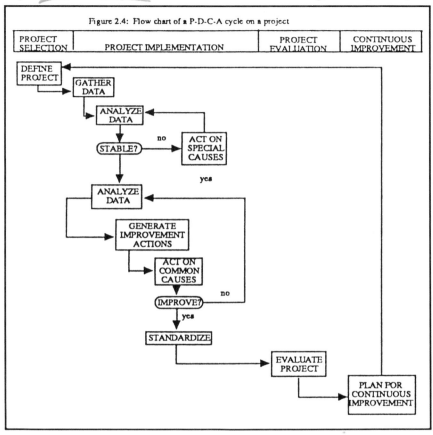

Figure 2.4: Flow chart of a P-D-C-A cycle on a project

As illustrated, a cross-functional project team has to gather and analyze data, and determine if its system is stable. If it is unstable, the team must stabilize the system before attempting to improve it. If the system is statistically stable, the team may recommend actions for improvement. The actions, once implemented, may require adjustments until the new system becomes stable. The project is evaluated and plans are made for continuous improvements.

One effective way to get input about the causes of identified problems in processes and systems is to post **cause-and-effect** diagrams, also known as fishbone charts and Ishikawa diagrams (Ishikawa 1982).

The use and benefits of these diagrams have been described by Sarazen (1990), who maintains that since most problems have more than one cause, the cause-and-effect diagram is useful in showing the relationships between a problem and multiple causes. They are most effective if the employees who contributed to the initial identification of a problem are asked by a cross-functional task force for their opinion of the causes. The four most common causes of problems are equipment, procedures, materials, and personnel. Examples of fishbone diagrams are shown in Figures 2.5 and 2.6.

Figure 2.5: An Ishikawa (cause-and-effect) diagram with main level 1 and level 2 causes

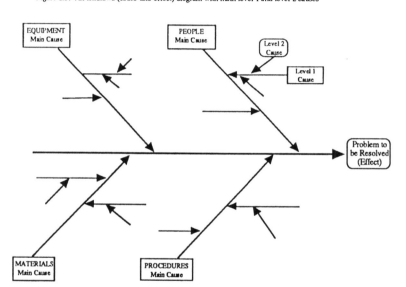

Figure 2.5 shows a cause-and-effect diagram with an undesirable identified effect. The effect, that is the problem needing to be resolved, could have been identified by the previously described nominal group process. As can be seen, the effect can have not only one or more main causes, but causes at several levels.

We are aware of a dean who displayed several 3 x 4 foot diagrams throughout departmental offices within her school when she identified that many faculty were receiving poor teaching evaluations by students. The sign had **Post-it** note pads attached so written remarks could be added by the faculty. At the end of several weeks, she gathered the information and shared it with all of the faculty via a memo. As a result, a task force was formed that began to address the entire faculty evaluation process which had become so routine it was ineffectual. We

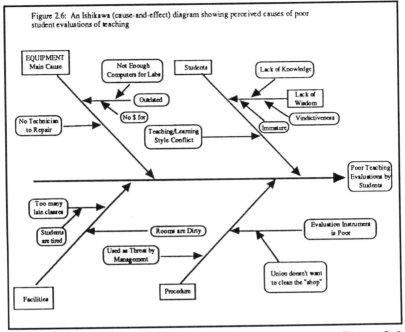

Figure 2.6: An Ishikawa (cause-and-effect) diagram showing perceived causes of poor student evaluations of teaching

have taken the liberty of sharing the dean's fishbone chart in Figure 2.6.

Case Study: Teaming for Quality

A Midwestern university faculty and administration determined that their teacher education students needed more contact with diverse cultures, and set out to make it happen. They established a series of meetings, engaged in a nominal group process to set curricular priorities and concluded that a student teaching experience in a Southern state with a large percentage of Hispanic students would meet their objectives. A senior faculty member with educational experience in the chosen region agreed to take charge of the program and conducted regular team meetings at the site and on campus. The program was publicized, attracted many students, resulted in superb professional opportunities for faculty who supervised student teachers, and received a national award as an innovative program. The program also provided outstanding experiences for students, many of whom accepted employment in the region. Periodically, they repeat the nominal group process to re-establish priorities and update their planning processes.

Customers and Suppliers

Each part of the college or university exists to do something, and that something is called its **product**. For whom it is done is called the **customer**. To perform a task the unit has **needs,** called **requirements**. The providers of the unit's needs are its **suppliers**. One unit's needs are another unit's product. Each combination of **do/need** is an interaction between a customer and a supplier.

To consider how the **customer/supplier** philosophy can be applied to higher education, we must examine references to business factors. The private sector is defined largely by the relationship between customers and suppliers, and by how the latter can use and improve production, distribution, and service systems to improve product quality and make and keep customers satisfied. Customer patronage is the object of competition among many firms. Each firm tries to maintain or increase market share by trying to please its customers, and survival depends upon repeat business. A central point in the quality leaders' philosophies involves viewing customers as part of the production line.

Higher education's concept of customers differs from the private sector's because there are no "repeat customers" in the usual sense. Students, once enrolled, tend to remain until they've received degrees. (Some may leave the institution but usually not because of dissatisfaction.) Except for education majors, alumni tend not to return to the same institution for additional degrees. It can be argued, however, that if alumni and current students are satisfied with their experience, they will recommend the institution to others. Likewise, employers who are well satisfied with the university's graduates may be disposed to hire additional graduates from the institution. Thus students, alumni, and employers share some characteristics of traditional customers.

A further parallel to the customer concept lies in the relationships among various components of a college or university. For example, virtually every operating unit is a "customer" of the maintenance department. Individual academic departments are customers of the dean's office, and *vice-versa*. An institution of higher education is a complex web of relationships, where any given person or office is both a customer and a supplier. The customer/supplier philosophy can be applied by concentrating on each unit of the institution in its role as a user of processes and systems to supply service to other units.

The customer/supplier relationship is very important if teamwork is to be effective. The institution must develop an appreciation of the concept to promote trust, pride, and quality. Central to applying the concept of quality into the classroom itself is an acceptance of the customer/supplier relationship!

Central to accepting the customer/supplier relationship as a prime condition for achieving TQI and TQM is the removal of the quasi-military model of management from colleges and universities. Instead, leadership training for all employees, including faculty and students, should be undertaken so everyone can reach their maximum performance. The decentralization necessary to stimulate a customer/supplier attitude requires a participative atmosphere. For this atmosphere to exist within our institutions, it's necessary to empower all employees, including students. With empowerment comes trust; with trust comes pride in workmanship; and with pride in workmanship comes teamwork for total quality improvement. An excellent reference for developing self-leadership skills has been published by Manz and Sims (1989).

Quality by Fact, Process, and Perception

Each of the quality leaders examines quality from at least three different perspectives: by fact (that is, does the product or service meet the specified requirements?); of process (does the process and/or system produce the product or service as intended?); and by perception (are customer expectations met?).

An institution could have quality by fact and of process, yet not have a perception of quality by customers, either graduates or employers of graduates. In this case, total quality has not been achieved. This is usually but **not always** the result of poor past performance, although poor marketing of new processes for improving quality can also contribute to the perception.

Case Study: Phasing out a Program

We are aware of an unusual situation where an associate degree program is being phased out even though it is of high quality by fact, of process, and by perception. This health related technical program has excellent faculty and state-of-the-art equipment and facilities, as well as the support of the administration, the professional community, and an active community advisory council. In addition, there are numerous employment opportunities for the program's graduates, and there are hardly any competing educational programs in the entire state. The administration and the faculty jointly pursued an aggressive advertising and promotion campaign, but enrollments continually dropped and the decision to close the program had to be made.

Although the program is of high quality in all respects, societal factors are against it. The graduates, although highly sought after, are poorly paid, and there is little chance for advancement in the profession. In addition, the profession does not have a credentialing body. In this particular state, high-school dropouts can be "trained" in a matter of months to do one or several of the tasks leading to the same end result. Apparently, society is willing to accept a lesser-quality end product.

Management by Fact

All leaders in the study of quality emphasize the need for complete and comprehensive data to make major decisions.

In determining an institution's mission or setting out to improve a simple process, one rule must apply: institutional research data should be complete and accurate, and made freely available to everyone. Information is useless if it's not available, and the free availability of information serves at least two purposes. First, when people know the facts, they are in a position to offer essential advice. They can call attention to a serious flaw in a developing plan. A flaw that is identified early and corrected can prevent **unnecessary expenditures**. Second, freely available information creates an atmosphere of trust that's essential for effective planning and high morale. Lack of information creates distrust.

Decisions should be based on data rather than hunches. Data and facts have a tendency to uncover the root of problems rather than the symptoms; thus, permanent solutions can be offered rather than quick fixes.

Case Study: Personnel Plan

A state university had experienced a nearly 30 percent enrollment increase over the past three years, but the provost was reluctant to ask the president for additional faculty positions. Apparently the provost was not convinced class sizes were optimal, when in fact, nearly all of the classrooms were filled to seating capacity, especially for general education courses. The deans presented their cases for additional faculty using a simple spreadsheet format, which identified the number of enrolled students and the faculty required when certain class sizes were maintained. For example, to teach X number of students, Y number of faculty are required if class sizes are Z.

Although the provost asked for additional information, his directions were confusing. This confusion, combined with his indecisiveness in approving either temporary or regular faculty, required the use of teaching overloads for regular faculty. This in turn not only decreased the grant writing and service effectiveness of the faculty, it decreased the working relationships between the faculty, chairpersons, deans, and the provost.

This is an example of using "request for data" as a delay tactic for not being able to make a decision when, in fact, the information was readily available from institutional research.

Complexity

All of the quality leaders realize that most processes and systems which produce a product or service are complex. Complexity can be defined, especially for institutions of higher education, as extra steps added to a process to deal with errors in the preceding process, or steps added to recover from errors occurring in the process.

There are four common types of complexity:

- **Mistakes/Defects:** Extra steps that are added to correct an error.
- **Breakdowns/Delays:** Lost time due to waiting for repair or rework.
- **Inefficiencies:** Excess time, material, or movement.
- **Variation:** Extra process steps to deal with excessive variability of inputs/outputs.

Case Study: New Employees

This case study is an excellent example of what can happen when Crosby's fourth, fifth, and sixth points are violated, and represents the four common mistakes in complexity mentioned above. This situation occurred at a Midwestern university.

Over the course of an academic year, a number of new employees arrived on campus, consisting of upper management and support positions, not faculty positions. They were not given the appropriate orientation, nor were they selected carefully. As a result, the deans and faculty complained to the president about the new employees' performance. In response, the president assigned these people to other jobs, again without on-the-job training. As a result, these employees performed poorly again. This scenario continued until each employee had been placed in about three different positions.

Since $700,000 was required to hire and reassign the upper-level managers and support staff, faculty members were denied raises because the president did not have available funds. He explained that these positions were necessary to accommodate an enrollment increase; however, he told the faculty they would receive salary increases in the following year.

The next year came and the faculty were informed they would receive no salary increase because it was necessary to hire new employees to replace the previously hired, reassigned employees. As before, the new employees were not trained for their positions and their performance was suspect. The president indicated, however, that they would not be released, but transferred to other positions to find appropriate employment. To make matters worse, student enrollment had stabilized.

In the third year the faculty were also denied raises, since the money was needed to support newly hired employees from the past two years. The faculty salary situation was exacerbated when state revenues were severely impacted by a recession and the university budget was reduced.

Variation

Every process involving machines and/or humans displays variation. In higher education, for example, we see wide variation in the incoming freshmen, in the teaching, and in the quality of graduates. Excessive variation, however, causes the processes and systems to be erratic and unpredictable, possibly resulting in poor quality.

Since every process shows variation, no two products — be they components, services, reports, teaching effectiveness, graduates — will ever be identical. The goal, therefore, is to improve the uniformity of the process. This can be done by getting everyone involved to study processes and identify potential sources of variation in an attempt to standardize processes and systems.

Once a process is in control, one can determine common cause and special cause variations by the use of simple statistics. Common cause variation is the inherent variation of a process that is the result of many small sources of variation. Special cause variation is a large, sporadic variation that is unusual to the process under study.

In summary, this chapter reviewed the common characteristics in the philosophies of the quality leaders, namely:

1. Processes and systems.

2. Teaming.

3. Customers and suppliers.

4. Quality by fact, process, and perception.

5. Management by fact.

6. Complexity.

7. Variation.

We also discussed how common characteristics could be applied to total quality improvement (TQI) and total quality management (TQM) of academic institutions. We introduced the nominal group process for identifying institutional problems causing poor quality, and the construction and use of Ishikawa (cause-and-effect) diagrams. We included case studies for emphasis and to illustrate management practices which hinder or enhance quality.

Chapter 3:
Determining Your Institution's Quality Index

This chapter suggests an expeditious method to obtain a baseline from which to begin a total quality improvement (TQI) program. The method uses a nationally recognized tool (from the Malcolm Baldrige Award) to evaluate an institution's quality index (QI). The suggested method can be used to rate either an entire institution or a single department/unit.

For this example, we assume that the president desires an overall assessment of the QI. We recommend that the president form three to five cross-functional teams of eight to 10, selected carefully and including members of the faculty, staff, and administration. Teams should also include students when they're involved in the management system (department committees, advisory committees, etc.).

For the method to work, teams should be fully informed and allowed adequate time for the exercise. They need a clear explanation of why the activity is taking place and how their candid and sincere opinions are essential to beginning a process toward TQI. If teams feel it's just a mindless activity serving no end, obviously they won't devote serious attention to the questions which, taken seriously, encourage discussion and occasional debate. Consequently, the matter of adequate time with a limit is important — allocate four hours for this exercise. From our experience it gives teams time for reflection and discussion while compelling them to reach difficult evaluations within the time limit.

We've modified the criteria in the Malcolm Baldrige Award categories for the following exercise. (The entire Malcolm Baldrige National Quality Award application package can be obtained from the National Institute of Standards and Technology at 301\975-2036.)

The categories are:

1. Leadership.
2. Information & analysis.
3. Planning for quality.
4. Human resource utilization.
5. Quality assurance of products and services.
6. Quality results.
7. Customer satisfaction.

As noted previously, these categories are recognized nationally as the key criteria for determining quality in manufacturing and service industries. We believe strongly that education is a service and its students customers; thus, a university or college should evaluate itself as other service industries do, especially as the challenge of foreign competition — in this case the comparatively high academic success of foreign schools and students — forces improvement here at home.

To begin the exercise, team members should read and discuss each of the categories and then, on a "Quality Index Rating Sheet" (a sample is shown at the end of this chapter), assign a score from 1 to 5 for each category or subcategory as indicated below. It's permissible to assign fractional equivalents, that is 2.5, 3.2, etc. Team members may wish to review the purpose and read through the categories before beginning the exercise, and should agree to or recognize a common objective to create a comfortable environment for reaching consensus throughout the exercise.

Category 1: Leadership (15 percent weight)

This category consists of three subcategories and examines primarily how the senior management (presidents, provosts, and deans) creates and sustains a clear, visible quality value and management system to guide the institution's activities. Fully informed team members should reflect on approaches and principles of TQM and TQI (Chapters 1 and 2) and discuss their presence or absence throughout the institution.

Assign points (1-5) for each category subsection based on the described criteria.

1.1. Describe what quality means to your institution. Does your institution have a formal statement on quality?

Points	Criteria
1	No formal statement.
2	Formal statement is focused on traditional characteristics, such as finest quality, zero mistakes, best value, etc.
3	Formal quality statement is in the mission statement, as well as departmental handbooks, brochures, etc.
4	All employees know what the formal statement on quality means to their department and the institution.
5	Formal statement relates to world-class quality results and continuous improvement in processes, systems, and education.

1.2   How has the quality policy and/or mission been deployed or spread throughout the institution?

Points	Criteria
1	Mainly "talk" about quality.
2	Have a quality manual.
3	Quality manual and/or policy statements about quality are distributed to the entire institution.
4	Workshops and/or seminars are routinely conducted on quality procedures and policy.
5	Quality policy is deployed to engender clear direction, commitment of people, and integration of separate activities

1.3   Describe management's leadership, personal involvement, and visibility through communication (speeches, publications, interviews) of quality inside and outside the institution to the community, region, state, and national organizations.

Points	Criteria
1	Traditional management role of directing, controlling and dictating what quality is and should be.
2	Management is visible in quality issues internally.
3	Management is visible in external quality issues as a means to demonstrate commitment.
4	Supports participative management within the entire organization and implements suggestions from quality circle groups. Is a cheerleader inside the institution and monitors group progress and improvement.
5	Recognized as a leader outside the institution for instituting quality.

Category 2: Information and Analysis (5 percent weight)

This category examines the scope, validity, use, and management of data that underlie the institution's total quality system. Adequacy of information supports a prevention-based quality approach using management by fact.

This is a key approach to TQI, and team members should review the "Management by Fact" section of Chapter 2 to foster informed discussion. Too often data and information systems are isolated, have limited accessibility and uncoordinated, even non-existent communication. In such environments people may not be aware that they have inadequate information. Their analysis, then, of quality issues — even those related to this category — suffers. Consequently, discussion and evaluation will greatly benefit from selecting team members across functional units in the institution.

Assign points (1-5) for this category based on the described criteria.

2.1   In what areas (such as accounting, recruiting, community service, employee satisfaction, student retention, graduates entering professional schools, number of errors, time for delivering a service, etc.) do you have data to illustrate quality trends by function and/or process?

Points	Criteria
1	No data, or just standard accounting data.
2	Standard retention, application to acceptance ratio, and re-do data.
3	Use of statistical methods to monitor critical processes and systems.
4	Cost of quality (COQ) analysis data available for all to examine.
5	All functions and departments/units collect and analyze statistical data and use a TQI process cycle to improve product/service quality.

Category 3: Strategic Quality Planning (5 percent weight)

This category examines the institution's planning process to meet its short and long-term goals, and to achieve or sustain a leadership position. Again, team members may wish to review Chapters 1 and 2 for background to discuss the institution's planning strategies. When the exercise is used to rate an entire institution, team members may discover that different departments use different strategies, and have to decide which will prevail. But when this category is used to rate a single department or division, evaluation should be much easier.

Assign points (1-5) for each category subsection based on the described criteria.

3.1 Summarize the institution's principal quality goals, objectives, and plans for the short-term (one to two years) and longer term (three to five years).

Points	Criteria
1	Standard management by objective (MBO), which keys on financial results or top management's goals.
2	Numerical objectives related to quality, cost effectiveness, and satisfaction.
3	Management by policy deployment where all faculty have quality work plan assignments related to the institution's mission.
4	Management by policy deployment, where all employees (faculty, staff, and managers) have quality work plan assignments related to the institution's mission.
5	The institution's objectives key on achieving world-class capabilities in quality related performance.

Category 4: Human Resource Utilization (15 percent weight)

This category examines the institution's effort to develop and utilize the work force's full potential for quality, and to maintain an environment conducive to full participation, continuous improvement, and personal growth. There are five subcategories to be considered.

Like Category 3, this will stimulate discussion and possibly debate when cross-functional teams rate an entire institution. The president may appoint a facilitator or hire a consultant to lead teams through the process, especially if areas of the institution are managed differently. We've witnessed group cohesion unravel at this point in the process, as questions can trigger cross-institutional rivalries and the natural competitiveness of human nature. Some managers may not be prepared for candid observations from clerical staff; clerical staff may be surprised to hear management's intentions, expressed candidly here and not in the administrative jargon of policy and procedures memoranda.

Many institutions will find Category 4 asking questions that have not been raised among employees before, and may feel the questions are loaded: "How can we be expected to educate employees in TQI," they might ask, "when we have just begun to consider it?" Frequently, without management directive, employees pursue these issues on their own, or divisions/departments choose to make quality a goal within delimited areas. We encourage teams to identify these efforts and quantify them; they will be important to long-term planning later.

Assign points (1-5) for each category subsection based on the described criteria.

4.1   What are the institution's key strategies for increasing employee effectiveness, productivity, and participation?

Points	Criteria
1	No institutional strategy.
2	Strategy is dependent on management's direction and efforts.
3	Participative management, which involves working on processes and systems.
4	Participative management, which empowers employees to make on-the-spot decisions.
5	Management is supportive of empowered employees' efforts; TGIF means "Thank God it's Fun" to work here: that is, employee morale is high.

4.2   Describe how the institution educates employees in TQI processes.

Points	Criteria
1	No employee education.
2	Employees educated on relevant job skills.
3	Employees educated on principles of quality.
4	Employees educated on principles of quality, including aspects of total quality improvement using statistical process control.
5	The keystone to training is the continuous improvement of all personnel.

4.3   What percentage of the current employees have ever received education in total quality improvement concepts?

Points	Criteria
1	0 percent.
2	Less than 25 percent.
3	25 to 60 percent.
4	61 to 90 percent.
5	91 to 100 percent.

4.4 Describe how the institution positively reinforces employees for contributions to quality improvement (such as recognition of teams, awards, etc.).

Points	Criteria
1	The rewards are either strictly monetary and arbitrarily disbursed, such as merit pay, or there is no formal program.
2	Typical performance review system which focuses on individual efforts.
3	Commendations and other non-monetary rewards that are dispensed by the judgment of management.
4	Commendations and other non-monetary rewards that are dispensed by the judgment of management, but with the input of at least two or more evaluators.
5	Team recognition and incentives for efforts based on improved processes and systems, where the manager's role was to support team efforts.

4.5 What has the institution done to ensure the quality of work life, maintain a supportive work environment, and empower all employees to actively participate?

Points	Criteria
1	Institution has a "do your job and leave your brains at home" environment.
2	Suggestion boxes available where suggestions are reviewed and discussed.
3	Participative management between faculty and administration.
4	Participative management with all employees involved.
5	Upside-down pyramid where managers lead and support personnel performing value-added work.

Category 5: Quality Assurance of Products and Services (15 percent weight)

This category examines the institution's systematic approach to producing quality products and services based primarily upon processes and systems, and including the control of procured materials, equipment, and services. There are four subcategories which address quality assurance of products and services. Team members should review the "Customer and Suppliers" and "Quality by Fact, Process and Perception" sections of Chapter 2 for discussion.

This category often challenges traditional conceptions of what higher education does. We strongly suggest that educational institutions adopt a new philosophy that conceives of education as a service, and the academic success of students as a product (which like other products can be tested and measured). The point may never be acceptable to those convinced otherwise. However, as the discussion turns to traditional products and services external and internal to the institution, team members should consider connections to the primary function of the college or university. Refusing to do so continues the past elitism of educators who wish to see their function as separate and privileged.

Assign points (1-5) for each category subsection based on the described criteria.

5.1   How does your institution define waste and what preventive measures is it taking to reduce waste?

Points	Criteria
1	No formal effort concerning "waste," such as the retention rate of students.
2	"Waste" is considered students who do not graduate, and is determined solely by inspection, such as written tests. Or "waste" is seen as "scrap" because the customer is not satisfied or the job has to be redone.
3	"Waste" includes measurable external failure costs, such as the cost of recruiting, advising, processing, and the expense of drop-outs to society.
4	Process orientation regarding "waste" is considered such as time, steps, complexity, loans, and scheduling and considers both internal and external costs.
5	"Waste" is recognized as a result of poor processes and systems, and includes all aspects of the educational process. Ongoing efforts utilizing group teams and cross-functional teams are employed routinely.

5.2   How does your institution improve quality to those supplying goods and services?

Points	Criteria
1	Purchasing is by contract specifications and goes to the lowest bidder.
2	Processes and systems track purchased items and data related to on-time delivery.
3	Suppliers (including high schools supplying students to the institution) are required to show quality control capabilities, otherwise stringent specifications are written and adhered to by various units/departments.
4	Institution has identified that the suppliers have process-oriented quality improvement capabilities.
5	Institution has an active partnership with suppliers to set and improve quality, price, and delivery. There is also combined training between the institution and suppliers, such as articulation agreements with community colleges and/or school districts.

5.3   How does your institution evaluate the quality of products and services provided by external sources?

Points	Criteria
1	No formal tracking program.
2	Reject tracking only: that is inspection upon delivery of goods.
3	Annual evaluation of suppliers' quality systems.
4	Active advisory committees between major suppliers and the institution.
5	Partnership and total performance teams in areas of quality, total cost, and on-time delivery. Suppliers are expected to improve continuously.

5.4   How does your institution evaluate the quality of products and services provided by people and departments inside your institution?

Points	Criteria
1	No institutional program available.
2	Institution has a committee working on establishing a program.

3   Each unit/department tracks its own quality indicators.

4   Institution has a culture that recognizes internal customer-supplier relationships.

5   Institution has a total quality improvement approach where the president audits the performance of processes and systems supporting the institution's mission.

Category 6: Quality Results (15 percent weight)

This category examines quality improvement based upon objective measures derived from customer requirements/expectations and operations analysis. Also examined are current quality levels in relation to those of competing organizations. Three subcategories comprise Quality Results.

"Quality Improvement" measurement at this early stage — collecting base-line data — may show no improvement or even declining performance. The purpose here is to get the baseline data, the starting point for measuring improvements later. Obviously, at this point analyzing the most objective data available best serves the exercise.

Assign points (1-5) for each category subsection based on the described criteria.

6.1 Construct a graph(s) showing key improvement data in your products and/or services, for example, graduation rates, the number of workshops requested by industry over the past five years, the increase in annual giving by alumni over the past five years, the number and percent of completed work orders by building and grounds over the past five years, etc.

Points	Criteria
1	Either no reliable data is available or just standard accounting data. Institutional graphs are generated only for special applications, such as a self-study report or a report to the governing board.
2	Traditional quality indicator information is used, such as the routine inspection of SAT/ACT scores of incoming freshmen. Information is supplied by either internal or external customers.
3	Traditional information is evaluated regularly in units/departments which use graphs that are understood by everyone in the unit/department.

4	Field intelligence data is gathered by the unit/department and is evaluated in graphical form. For example, the number or percent of those in the top 10 percent of the graduating class that came from a given school district, the percentage of purchase orders that are processed within three working days, etc.
5	Information related to strategic quality objectives are regularly used and are posted in graphical form throughout the institution for all to see.

6.2 Briefly describe one or two continuous improvement project(s) which have led to the results in 6.1.

Points	Criteria
1	Institution has no project teams or no measurable results available.
2	Project teams or committees are put together quickly to examine the special cause effects.
3	Management appoints standard committees to address such issues as enrollment, cost of instruction, general education, remodeling of facilities/classrooms, etc.
4	Management appoints mandatory project teams to study areas needing improvement. Management almost always implements the team's recommendations.
5	Management appoints mandatory project teams to study issues related to quality and value-added work that have measurable results. The main work, using quality tools and methods, is done by front-line personnel (It is common for such places to have quality stories.)

6.3 Describe how you compare yourself with other institutions within or outside your service area (benchmarking).

Points	Criteria
1	Institution has no comparable data available.
2	Standard accounting information, such as profits, return on assets, number of FTE or headcount, student to faculty ratio, etc.
3	Passive collection and analysis of data from outside sources, such as the alumni association.

4   Benchmarking of competitors, for example, the percentage of graduates from your institution going on to professional schools compared to other institutions in your region.

5   Institution has active program to obtain comparative "benchmarking" data on all functions and services from the *best* in those areas, whether competitors or not.

Category 7: Customer Satisfaction (30 percent weight)

This category examines the institution's knowledge of the customer, the overall customer service system, and the ability to meet customer requirements and expectations. Again, this category, like Category 6, requires team members to conceive of high schools, employers, students, and alumni as customers.

Testing customer satisfaction is a key element of quality improvement, and teams will have to decide whose satisfaction should be measured: if not students, then alumni; if not high schools, then employers. Regardless how the "customer" is defined, institutions of higher education must test their performance by measuring the opinions of the public they serve. For some institutions, that public is narrowly defined; for others it may be widely defined, including taxpayers, trustees, legislators, and special interest groups.

Assign points (1-5) for each category subsection based on the described criteria.

7.1   How does your institution determine who external customers are and their satisfaction level?

Points	Criteria
1	Institution has no formal collection systems to measure external customer satisfaction. All information is hearsay, such as enrollments are doing OK so we must be OK.
2	A complaint follow-up process is in place.
3	A formal complaint handling system provides feedback to appropriate areas. Complaints are treated as "special causes."
4	A TQI process is used with information gathered from customer (alumni, faculty, secretaries, students, etc.) satisfaction surveys. The processes monitor key indicators of customer satisfaction.
5	Institution has a comprehensive data collection system that leads to Quality Function Deployment for products and services.

7.2   How do you determine who your internal customers are and their satisfaction levels?

Points	Criteria
1	No formal program exists at the institution.
2	Communication of satisfaction is channeled mainly through management hierarchy.
3	Cross functional teams are deployed routinely to determine satisfaction though surveys.
4	Cross functional teams are deployed routinely to determine satisfaction though surveys. Then a TQI process, such as the P-D-C-A cycle, is used to improve the internal customer-supplier relationship.
5	All functions are engaged in TQI processes for internal customer satisfaction. Team communications are horizontal.

7.3   In what areas, processes, or systems does your institution have defined, measurable product and/or service quality criteria?

Points	Criteria
1	None.
2	Management measures certain products or services.
3	Management measures at least 50 percent of the products or services.
4	Management and employees measure at least 50 percent of the products or services.
5	The institution has a total quality system oriented toward data gathering.

7.4   What methods does your institution use to determine customer satisfaction?

Points	Criteria
1	No analysis is done.
2	Some tracking of passively gathered data.
3	Regular tracking of passively gathered data.

4	Active accumulation and analysis of customer satisfaction data.
5	The entire institution is actively involved with all internal and external customer satisfaction measures. Persons who perform the service, such as faculty, talk to graduates and/or their employers several years after graduation to gather information.

7.5 Summarize trends in customer satisfaction and list measurements your institution has in specific areas.

Points	Criteria
1	Institution has no applicable information.
2	Information is just hearsay, such as more people use our unit than the past, so we must be doing OK.
3	Specific measurable data is available through external sources, such as employers or alumni groups, showing improved customer satisfaction with the institution.
4	The Office of Institutional Research constantly produces statistically valid questionnaires and mails them to various groups to determine trends.
5	The institution specifically generates and monitors data which evaluates key quality criteria to determine constant year-to-year improvements.

7.6 What does your institution do that significantly promotes continuous improvements of customer satisfaction?

Points	Criteria
1	Nothing.
2	Quality successes are recognized with awards, certification, accreditation, etc.
3	In addition to recognition awards, the president sends kudos personally to the person/unit.
4	The institution has undergone TQI and TQM training and has shown improvement.
5	The institution has become actively involved in the Quality Movement locally and nationally. The institution has published papers and/or made speeches about the quality of their processes and systems.

Please enter your results on the following rating sheet and perform the calculations.

Quality Index Rating Sheet

Institution:_____

Reviewer(s):_____

Date:_____ Document notes, questions, etc. on reverse side.

Note: All ratings are from 1-5.

1.0 Leadership

1.1 _____

1.2 _____

1.3 _____

Total divided by 3 x 0.15 _____

2.0 Information & Analysis

2.1 _____

Total x 0.05 _____

3.0 Quality Planning

3.1 _____

Total x 0.05 _____

4.0 Human Resource Utilization

4.1 _____

4.2 _____

4.3 _____

4.4 _____

4.5 _____

Total divided by 5 x 0.15 _____

5.0 Quality of Products & Services

5.1 _____

5.2 _____

5.3 _____

5.4 _____

Total divided by 4 x 0.15 _____

6.0 Quality Results

6.1 _____

6.2 _____

6.3 _____

Total divided by 3 x 0.15 _____

7.0 Customer Satisfaction

7.1 _____

7.2 _____

7.3 _____

7.4 _____

7.5 _____

7.6 _____

Total divided by 6 x 0.30 _____

Quality Index = Sum of Weighted Totals from 1.0 to 7.0 _____

In the previous rating and scoring procedure we suggest the following categories:

Quality Index	Category	Description
0 to 2.9	I	Substantial improvement in TQI education required.
3.0 to 3.4	II	Commitment toward TQI.
3.5 to 3.9	III	Progress toward TQI.
4.0 to 5.0	IV	Achievement of TQI.

This exercise gives a rough indication of an institution's quality index as determined by our modification of the Malcolm Baldrige Award criteria. We've used this rating and scoring process at a number of workshops which were attended by representatives from community colleges, private liberal arts colleges and universities, comprehensive universities, private and public research universities, and an armed force academy. In all instances, participants agreed that their final QI score reflected their institutional quality.

After an institution rates its QI, the president and top management may wish to establish TQM education and training sessions and implement a TQI movement for the entire institution.

If the results indicate a substantial, measurable improvement in the QI, the president may wish to submit an application for the Malcolm Baldrige Award. There are a number of seminars that offer training sessions on how to complete this application (American Society for Quality Control, 310 West Wisconsin Avenue, Milwaukee, WI 53203).

Chapter 4:
Five Necessary Conditions for Implementing TQM and TQI in Academic Institutions

The purpose of this chapter is to elaborate on the conditions necessary for establishing a total quality culture in colleges and universities. Although we've borrowed extensively from the quality leaders, we have not promoted a single philosophy, such as Deming's or Crosby's. Individual institutions may wish to use key points from all the theorists or develop their own philosophy based on the principles specified in Chapter 2. We believe, however, that institutions wishing to adopt a new approach, emphasizing quality, can do so by adopting a clear focus on the conditions necessary for change.

The following five conditions for implementing TQM and TQI should be established sequentially, rather than at random:

Condition One: Education and administrative commitment.

Condition Two: Education and commitment of faculty and staff.

Condition Three: Establish trust.

Condition Four: Establish pride in workmanship.

Condition Five: Change the institutional culture.

Let us elaborate on each of the conditions.

Condition One: Education and Administrative Commitment

All of the quality leaders make the point that before lasting change toward quality can be realized, management must: (1) be trained in quality processes and systems, and (2) make it clear that they will support the commitment toward quality. Remember the quality commitment that guides the work of all employees at Philip Crosby Associates, which we referred to in Chapter 2:

> *We will perform defect-free work for our clients and our associates. We will fully understand the requirements for our jobs and the systems that support us. We will conform to those requirements at all times* (Crosby 1984, p. 103).

Few college presidents could make similar statements about their institutions. How many presidents, vice presidents, and deans in institutions of higher education are even knowledgeable about quality processes and systems? Obviously, if administrators are not educated in the principles of TQM and TQI, how can they be expected to make a total commitment? Therefore, a correct start is crucial for the implementation of TQM and TQI, and the correct start is the education and commitment of the administration.

Since implementing TQM and TQI requires an enormous deviation from how most managers supervise in universities and colleges, the president and her or his top managers should undergo a training program on the principles of TQM and TQI. Then, similar training must be provided to middle managers. After all managers have undergone the educational experience, the president should consider the following:

Make it known that TQM and TQI are not being tested as concepts, but that the commitment to proceed with them is genuine. In fact, the president must consistently "walk the talk" on TQM/TQI, and let it be known that the only question is how to best implement quality throughout the institution. As pointed out by Peters and Austin in *A Passion for Excellence* (1985) *Attention to quality can become the organization's mind-set only if all of its managers —indeed, all of its people —live it.* They stress that "living it" means paying attention to quality 100 percent of the time and not allowing lapses now and then.

Release or reassign managers that disagree with the movement, even though they might represent 25 to 33 percent of the management team. If this needs to be done, it will become obvious that the movement for TQM and TQI is real, and if senior executives don't support it with words and action, they will be replaced. This also sends the signal that management is responsible for not only identifying problems in processes and systems but for maintaining and improving quality as well.

Appoint a vice president of quality who reports directly to the president. This person should have extensive experience as both a faculty member and an administrator in an educational institution. In addition, the person needs to be completely familiar with the principles and procedures of TQM and TQI. Her or his job description should include the following duties:

- Develop and teach quality awareness programs for all personnel.

- Constantly survey employees as to task, process, and system problems requiring improvement.

- Educate total quality councils appointed by the president, as well as the community advisory council, and members of the governing board.

- Promote the customer/supplier concept throughout the institution.

- Meet with external "customers" to understand their perceptions of the institution.

- Encourage the integration of process and system designs with emphasis on error-free processes.

- Ensure adequate allocation of resources to properly meet process and system requirements.

- Establish detection methods that point out process and system errors, rather than product or people defects.

- Establish benchmarking and statistical techniques for the various divisions/units.

- Coordinate the development of the institution's long-term strategy toward TQM and TQI.

- Publish a newsletter that communicates TQI successes.

- Post graphs and charts showing TQI trends for various departments/units.

Appointing a TQM community advisory council is important because many members can be considered **suppliers** (such as high school educators), whereas others can be considered **customers** (such as employers of the graduates), and still others as **consumers** (such as the parents of students or even the students themselves). Too often members of this group have difficulty working together since they all will admit they want **quality** but have no background in TQM or TQI. By bringing the external groups with their varying perspectives together, the group not only acts as a barometer of public opinion about the institution, but also provides valuable information as how better to market the institution's efforts towards TQM and TQI.

Imagine the reaction of a high school principal, who is not educated in TQM and TQI and is a member of a Total Quality Community Advisory Council, when she or he is told there is a high rejection ratio of applicants from her or his school because:

1. Applicants don't meet entrance requirements.

2. Applicants who are admitted have marginal qualifications to succeed, as measured by a variety of tests.

3. Fifty percent of the students who are admitted require remedial courses.

4. Sixty percent of the students who are admitted either fail or drop out.

5.   It costs more to educate students from her or his institution than other institutions.

Likewise, imagine the reaction of a college/university's vice presidents, deans, chairpersons, and faculty who, trained or not in TQM and TQI, are informed that the reasons regional industries either don't employ or reluctantly employ their graduates include:

1.   Graduates don't meet the specifications for entry.
2.   Graduates who are employed have marginal qualifications to succeed.
3.   Fifty percent of the graduates who are employed require remedial training to bring them up to speed.
4.   Sixty percent of the graduates who are employed either quit or are fired within four years.
5.   It costs more to employ their graduates than those from other institutions.

Confronted with such information, educators initially respond emotionally, as though their personal credentials are challenged, and in denial resist adopting quality changes.

After the appropriate education in TQM and TQI, however, these problems are looked upon and examined from a process and system approach, rather than a personal or emotional approach. Then, and only then, can progress be made toward a solution.

Further examination of these typical cases reveals that in both there should have been an increase in the supplier's awareness of the importance of quality to the customer. In the first case the customer was the college; in the second case the customer was the employer of the college graduate. Here are examples of several possible outcomes of the community advisory council after receiving training in TQM and TQI:

- 1. Customers can have regular meetings with suppliers to foster and understand each other's needs and requirements.
- 2. The suppliers, on the other hand, are constantly informed as to how they are performing in meeting those needs.

The process by which these groups learn to evaluate the problems listed above in the "supplier/customer" system takes a long time. It is an ongoing, educational process for all members of the council. Overcoming the emotional response to the failure of systems is hard to do — we don't suggest otherwise. To overcome that difficulty, however, we emphasize the need for extensive training for all administrators, objective examination of systems and work habits, and finally, a dedication to the advancement of the institution's mission, not its bureaucracy.

Appoint a TQI council for each department/unit/division. The council for an academic area should consist of department chairpersons and the dean. Councils should be expected to hold regular meetings that are devoted entirely to TQI, and should be required to report monthly to the vice president of quality on their achievements. Quality meetings should be as important as budget meetings, curricular meetings, and evaluation meetings.

Total quality councils should be expected to:

1. Focus the unit's quality processes toward desired objectives that are consistent with the institution's mission and long-range goals.
2. Ensure that TQI and TQM education is adequate and ongoing.
3. Do continual reviews and benchmarking, and display quality improvement trends in forms of graphs and charts.
4. Constantly prioritize and update, via the nominal group procedure, tasks, processes, and systems that add to the cost of non-quality.
5. Encourage employee participation in quality circles.
6. Recognize quality improvements internally and externally.
7. Identify and correct tasks, processes, and systems that detract from a total quality education and/or experience.

The council for an academic area should consist of department chairpersons and the dean. All councils should hold regular meetings that are devoted entirely to TQI, and report monthly to the vice president of quality.

Encourage members of the institution's Governing Board to participate in TQM and TQI seminars. This usually requires an in-depth session at least once a year. This is necessary, as most members of governing boards come from the traditional settings of business and education which are, by nature, bureaucratic. Consequently, they are usually, but not always, highly conservative and tend to avoid experimentation, as experimentation means mistakes. Mistakes, of course, occur in all institutions, and the usual reaction in highly bureaucratic institutions is to place blame on subordinates rather than examine the system. The latter activity would more likely reveal the source of the problem.

When a governing board becomes convinced of the efficacy of the TQM and TQI movement, it serves not only as an ardent supporter but an advocate with the community and the legislature about the sincere efforts. This support could lead to an increased funding. In fact, we're aware of several prominent governing board members who took the initiative to convince administrators at their particular educational institutions to institute TQM and TQI.

Insist that management write a quality philosophy guidebook for all employees. Later, they will use the guidebook as they develop TQI processes and systems for their department/unit. This should be coordinated by the vice president for quality as a "work-in-progress." It gives employees a text which they can refer to and revise, and moreover, it gives them the important sense of participating in the process rather than being subjects to a process.

Establish a TQI Center with its own staff who report directly to the vice president of quality. This is a strategic move, as it makes obvious to the internal and external community that quality is important. The Total Quality Improvement Center can: (1) act as the educational arm for the administration, faculty, and staff; (2) coordinate continuing education activities for external agencies requesting training on quality improvement techniques, such as statistical process control; (3) act as a broker between the institution and the community it serves; (4) act as a conduit for quality research activities for not only the institution (faculty, administrators, staff), but also the community the institution serves; (5) help faculty develop quality teaching strategies; and, (6) educate the institution's suppliers and independent contractors.

Progress toward TQM and TQI must begin with the support of top management, since that group controls resource allocation. If top management sets an example for the rest of the institution, deans, chairpersons, and directors will soon recognize the movement is authentic and not just the latest fad. Managers who feel threatened by TQM empowerment procedures and who do not comply with TQI guidelines will have to be replaced. This will send a strong signal to the entire institution about the president's commitment to total quality. The faculty and staff will eventually accept the fact that the TQM and TQI movements are not just another method to improve productivity, but a very real commitment toward **quality**.

Top managers must serve as models for the commitment to quality. Otherwise, deans and chairpersons will not fully support TQM, and the faculty and staff will not spend much time on TQI if they feel quality is not a priority. Top management commitment must be inarguable.

To emphasize the importance of quality, the institution president should: (1) make quality improvement an agenda item at performance evaluation meetings with the vice presidents and deans, and (2) include the establishment and measurement of quality goals in the institutional mission statement and master plan. Of course, include faculty and staff when establishing the long-range plan and revising the mission statement.

We know of one highly successful president who meets with his vice presidents, deans, and staff first thing every Monday morning and asks them, "What are you going to do this week to improve quality and make this university a better place to work?" At this institution everybody must attempt to improve a task or process. Failure is not admonished but not trying to improve something is. Then the president meets with the same group every Friday afternoon and asks for a brief progress report. Obviously, the institutional culture at this university is one of constant attention to quality and change.

Administrators must realize that by launching an institution toward TQM and TQI there will be much distrust from the faculty and staff, who may feel threatened by the action. They may look upon the action as one designed to increase productivity under the rubric of total quality improvement. But the process of establishing trust must be open-ended, with no time commitment established by management. It takes time to establish trust, but when it is established, pride-in-workmanship and improvement in quality results. Eventually, a new institutional culture will be established. The importance of **trust** is discussed in Condition Three; **pride-in-workmanship** in Condition Four; and **changing the institutional culture** in Condition Five.

Condition Two: Education and Commitment of Faculty and Staff

Critical to the success of TQM and TQI is the education of not only managers, but the faculty and staff as well. Once the faculty and staff understand the principles of TQM and TQI, they will commit to the movement, even if only in incremental amounts. The education of faculty and staff should include an understanding of quality philosophies and processes, as well as training on the tools and techniques they'll need to implement TQI. After the initial sessions on TQI and TQM principles, it's necessary to separate the various groups and tailor the programs for each unit, such as the academic departments, accounting department, continuing education unit, police department, building and grounds, etc.

The obvious reason for educating the employees on TQM and TQI is to inform them that their participation is essential for the processes to work. After they realize the TQI movement is not just another management tool to increase productivity, that their contributions are respected and their roles in improving quality are essential, most employees will make a commitment. Otherwise, after they receive training, employees return to the office and all too frequently discover they cannot change systems and processes because they don't have the necessary resources or support to implement what they have learned. This can only lead to employee frustration and ensure the failure of the TQM and TQI movement.

Case Study: Task Force 1

The management and employees of a particular institution had undergone extensive training in TQM and TQI and were very excited about implementing some of the procedures. Upon returning to the institution, the president formed a cross-functional group called Task Force 1 (for the first problem to be addressed by TQI procedures) to address one of the top problems contributing to non-quality. The problem was identified by the nominal group process technique. The task force members used the P-D-C-A model, and after several months of hard work, made five key suggestions for improving system processes that were causing an enormous amount of waste. The president acknowledged receipt of the report, but neither implemented the suggestions nor gave reasons as to why he did not take the advice of the Task Force 1. Morale plummeted. People returned to the old way of doing things. Several months later, the president tried to form Task Force 2 but could not find any non-managers to participate. As a result, the "we-versus-them" attitude returned to this institution despite initial efforts to adopt a new philosophy.

Condition Three: Establish Trust

Since one of the main functions of TQM and TQI is to show constant improvement in the quality of service and product delivered, all departments must gather baseline data and take measurements on various operations over time. Gathering data and pointing out defects may threaten employees at first, and the only way to overcome the perceived threat is to establish trust. This may take time in institutions having poor records of collegiality. **Note, however, that only management can extend the offering of empowerment and trust since it controls 85 to 95 percent of the processes and systems in which employees work.**

The establishment of trust must not be dependent on time, it has to be dependent on results based on long-term relationships in establishing quality.

When trust exists, faculty and staff will feel empowered and they will have greater control of their job functions, making their positions more efficient. When this occurs, the working day goes quickly and people feel good about working for the institution.

Empowerment and trust also encourage employees to conduct self-directed assessment and constantly improve job performance so work can be done quicker, better, and at a lesser cost.

If the definition of empowerment is accepted as *a process of enhancing feelings of self-efficacy among organizational members through the identification of conditions that foster powerlessness and through their removal by both formal organizational practices and informal techniques of providing efficacy information,* (Conger and Kanungo, 1988) then one can extend trust to the individual. Trust and empowerment, therefore, are more than participative management; they are directly involved in self-leadership skill development where people make decisions and take action on the best way to solve problems — especially job-related problems. If people feel powerless, on the other hand, they will do as little as possible to maintain their jobs. Quality will be valued to the lowest common denominator.

The first thing that needs to be done to establish trust is to explain in detail why comprehensive measurements have to be taken. Explanations should show how data can: (1) demonstrate trends in customer satisfaction levels, including their satisfaction with the administration and other departments/units; (2) determine if the institution is meeting its mission and quality goals; (3) reveal to the state legislators that the institution is improving its efficiency and productivity; and (4) let employees know how well they and their units/departments are doing.

Second, inform employees that most of the measurements will be done by their departments/units and will be relevant to their needs, as well as the needs of their customers. They should also be informed that the measurements will be simple, understandable, and few in number. Measurements will be taken by all departments and divisions, beginning with top management (if not previously done). Because gathering baseline data is a valuable means of taking pictures of the system to measure improvement, it must include all parts of the organization. Otherwise later, management may face the accusation that because it did not make noticeable changes, improvements in other parts of the company/organization were hindered.

Third, employees must see that the commitment made by management is more than a "club" culture. In addition to replacing managers who do not comply with TQI procedures, those who are retained must actively and enthusiastically participate in the same kinds of self-examination required of employees. Managers must be involved in measuring their own effectiveness and making honest judgments from the data. In some cases this will be job- or tenure-threatening to a manager or group of managers. The situation is most likely one in which sooner or later the university or college would have to retrench or trim that part of the administrative bureaucracy. If management is truly going to establish trust, it must face the inevitable restructuring of itself in a timely, straightforward manner.

Instead of control, trust is the main item that must be established to make the institution a place where working relationships can flourish. People cannot feel like robots; they must flourish and have fun in their work. Of course, trust involves a gamble. According to Levering (1988, p. 188) *trust is... a calculated risk made with one's eyes open to the possibilities of failure, but it is extended with the expectation of success.* In places with poor management-union relationships, one can almost always be sure that lack of trust is a main reason.

When trust exists, faculty and staff will realize that management really respects their opinions. This is also true of middle managers caught between the faculty/staff and the top managers, especially deans and department chairpersons. As a result of **trust,** employees will feel empowered to take corrective action on poor processes, and will feel free to be authentic and express their true feelings about the tasks, processes, and systems which need attention for the institution to demonstrate constant improvement.

If, instead, trust is undermined by the "greed" factor, employees do nothing outside of their job description for which they are not compensated. TQM enables managers to counter the contract mentality by emphasizing the benefit of the educational process, and the enhanced marketability of the employee for having gained additional skills. In a "commodity-like" exchange where both management and faculty/staff give up something *roughly equivalent in value* (Levering, p. 194), quality cannot be a goal because each side is committed to an outmoded reward/punishment syndrome. With this understanding, if the employee does not perform as expected, management makes an "adjustment," and the employee is punished.

More preferable to that situation is management extending **trust** in a "giftlike" fashion (Levering, p. 197). Then, the faculty/staff member must either reject it or give up something for the common goal of TQI. If the faculty/staff member betrays the trust, powerful peer pressure will be exerted.

Case Study: *Control Within Controls*

During a retreat, a university president announced to his vice presidents and deans that it was their duty to design their personal performance objectives by his objectives, and that their objectives were to be fully supportive of his goals and philosophy. They were informed that only he knew what was best for the university. They were also told that they were to only act as a sender and receiver of information between the faculty and staff and him, and that they were to relay his orders/goals/objectives to them. Managers were expected to avoid friendships with the faculty and staff, as it would jaundice their management perspective of the institution's mission. Needless to say, collegiality did not exist in this institution, and the president's leadership abilities were suspect, even among his closest managers. This is a classic example of the misuse of **MBO**, and the results-oriented Taylor philosophy of "leave your brains at home, I hired a body."

Some suggest that it takes three to six years or longer to establish trust and empowerment in an institution. This may be true; however, if trust and empowerment are focused on initial TQI projects, faculty and staff will participate actively in the actual implementation of TQI. For this to occur, management must treat trust and empowerment as an evolutionary process, by getting faculty and staff involved initially in processes that show respect and trust for their knowledge and judgment — such as using the nominal group process to direct unit planning. As faculty and staff become more involved — by virtue of feeling trusted and empowered — in changing system processes, management must focus more of its attention on trust and empowerment. This involves educating employees in TQM and TQI, as mentioned in Condition Two, and applying the **adhocracy** procedures as discussed by Waterman (1990). Among his suggestions for instituting participative management are:

1. Get the right start.
2. Action.
3. Get results.

Get the right start includes getting managers, faculty and staff involved immediately after they have been educated in TQM and TQI. This is best accomplished by selecting a project team and a project which requires "fixing" processes and systems so an improvement in quality can be measured effectively. The chairperson of the cross-functional team should not be the perceived expert (Waterman 1990, p. 23), nor should the chairperson be a manager. The team should consist of 10 or fewer people and should represent as many units that are affected by its work. After the project team is formed, it must have:

- Consistent management support.
- Baseline data to demonstrate improvements.
- Time for regular meetings.
- Recognition of team success and efforts.

Action means "do it." It means examining baseline data and measuring the cost of nonconformance. It means defining problems and examining alternatives. Eventually it may mean making suggestions that are innovative and totally new — suggestions that may make the faculty, staff, and administration uncomfortable, as no one likes potential failure(s). Action also means that the project team be given the proper support for it to meet, deliberate, and draw up reports. Action means that the administration implements, to the greatest extent possible, every suggestion made by the team. Action means measuring the results of the modified process and/or system and rewarding the team if improvement occurs, but not punishing the team if there is no improvement. After all, it is far better to have tried and failed, than not to have tried anything.

Getting results, according to Waterman (p. 55), is implementing change. Like most American institutions, colleges and universities typically plan well, but are deficient at implementing plans. A good example is the practice of most academic institutions of forming long-range plans and mission statements that are not directly tied to the budgeting process. In fact, we're aware of several universities who diligently produce a master plan six months *after* the actual budget allocation process. In addition, the master plan had no relation to the allocated budget! It is no wonder, therefore, that most institutions have difficulty implementing even the most basic action plan that requires the allocation of resources. Waterman (1990, p. 57) states that *he has seen this happen again and again. First rate people. Excellent analysis. Solid recommendations. Token implementation.*

These three steps, along with establishing trust and empowering employees, will crystallize the implementation of participative management within an institution. If properly nurtured with continuous education in TQI, participative management should help faculty and staff identify poor processes and systems, and make better decisions and/or recommendations of how to solve problems and make improvements. In addition, empowered employees feel better about themselves as they develop their skills to a fuller extent. This will result in greater job satisfaction, better morale and improved productivity and quality.

Without trust and empowerment, participative management cannot exist. What does exist is a *pushy, controlling, directive management style* (Waterman, p. 23). The end result is a death sentence for quality.

Case Study: Respect as a Prerequisite for Trust

A vice president for academic affairs at a small Midwestern private university took seriously the anger of the faculty about administrative vetoes of what the faculty considered to be well-considered and well-planned curricular proposals. He quickly realized and shared his concern with the president that faculty felt like pawns in game of chess played by the president and his administrative team. To his credit, the president established a series of meetings where he and his administrative staff listened intently to faculty concerns. After the meetings, he established a Council of Faculty Advisors who regularly updated him on faculty concerns and made recommendations for empowering the faculty to take more responsibility for their jobs. He accepted 90 percent of their suggestions and took the calculated risk that faculty would make sure their recommendations were effectively implemented. Once faculty members realized the president and his staff trusted them to make recommendations in the interest of students and the instructional program, they took a more active part in all university activities, and the quality of their recommendations improved. The chairperson of the Council of Faculty Advisors soon became a member of the president's cabinet with full voting rights and the membership privileges. This gave the chair an intimate view of the workings of the administration and an opportunity to influence decisions in the making. Fear of the unknown was eliminated and a realization of the difficult decisions facing the president's cabinet was increased.

Case Study: Determining Class Sizes

At a state university, the unionized faculty were complaining that class sizes were much too large for them to assess students appropriately. The faculty also said they could teach only by the lecture method, since the classes were much too large for meaningful discussion to take place.

The administration claimed correctly that they had the right to determine class sizes, and that they had to be responsible to taxpayers in two specific areas, namely productivity and quality.

When we examined this institution's data, we noticed that the retention rate of baccalaureate degree-seeking students was only 40 percent; that the upper division courses in most majors were under subscribed; and that the students were being assessed mainly by examinations that were easily corrected, that is, true/false, multiple choice, etc. In addition, the class size issue resulted in bitter feelings between the faculty and the administration.

Shortly after being hired, a new vice president for academic affairs (VPAA) got the **right start, action, and results** using the procedures described above.

Get the right start: He requested that school deans, with their respective chairpersons, mutually agree on class sizes for each course, and submit their recommendations to him within six months. In determining class sizes, the deans and chairpersons were given data on previous class sizes. They were to gather the baseline data as to the preferred teaching style (lecture, discussion, seminar) of each professor, determine how each professor assessed students, and how they would assess students differently if class sizes were reduced.

Action: The task force recommended that class sizes should be reduced from 50 to 35 students in many general education classes and in many courses taken by freshmen. (This is known as "front loading.") The VPAA agreed, provided the chairpersons and the deans could demonstrate better assessments were taking place. They agreed. They were empowered to lower class sizes. Trust prevailed.

Get results: As a result of implementing the task force's suggestions, the following benefits were noticed three years later:

Chairpersons, faculty, and deans worked together to eliminate many courses that were not necessary for majors but which crept into the offerings over the past 30 years. In fact, the number of FTE faculty positions required to teach these courses were 15 (out of 350 faculty members). This resulted in the university being able to offer more sections of courses that were in high demand without reverting to overload or additional hiring.

As a result of better testing, advising, etc., student retention rates increased 30 percent. This resulted in more students for upper-division courses, and the overall cost per student credit hour was, in fact, decreased significantly over the years when the freshmen classes were considerably larger! For those faculty that did not honor the trust agreement, their class sizes were returned to the original level.

Condition Four: Establish Pride in Workmanship

Educating and empowering faculty, staff, and managers in TQM and TQI procedures, appointing project task forces, and participative goal setting will accomplish much in improving the quality of education. Nevertheless, too many times presidents and deans promise the legislatures and the public that the students from their institution are receiving a high-quality education, when in fact, they are not. Many of our colleges and universities do not have the state-of-the-art equipment that graduates will be expected to use in the work force. As a result, many professors in the sciences are significantly limited in the educational quality they can deliver. In fact, many science professors in lower-tier institutions are forced to offer very narrow laboratory experiences because they lack supplies, equipment, and resources. In some cases, college laboratories are less equipped than those in high schools. Furthermore, it is the job of the administration to provide the faculty with the supplies, resources, and equipment necessary to offer high-quality educational experiences. As Deming states in his 12th point, management must "**Remove barriers that rob employees of their right to pride in workmanship**" (p. 23). While management seeks the funds for obtaining supplies and equipment, it must not penalize faculty and staff in the benchmarking procedure by comparing them to counterparts at well-equipped research universities. Otherwise, the faculty and staff may never be recognized and rewarded for their efforts.

State-of-the-art equipment does not in itself improve the quality of the educational experience, but having it does remove certain barriers.

Employee trust is one outcome of a no-holds-barred crusade toward improving the processes and systems for quality results. Empowered employees begin to improve processes and systems and contribute significantly to improving quality. When they are rewarded and recognized for their efforts, they have greater pride in workmanship. A good reward and recognition program is an essential catalyst for involving everyone in TQI and changing the institutional culture.

In *Eleven Conditions of Excellence: The IBM Total Quality Improvement Process,* Ray F. Boedecker (1989, pp. 189-212) discusses the excellent rewards and recognition program that exists at IBM. He notes the following benefits of the program:

1. It emphasizes the importance management ascribes to quality.

2. It offers a highly visible forum to thank achievers.
3. It provides employees with goals.
4. It boosts morale and fosters friendly competition.
5. It can help in participative management efforts.

Although we do not subscribe to the practice of offering monetary rewards for improvements in quality, we support other forms of rewards and recognition. We mentioned the efforts of one school where a quality recognition and award ceremony is held with success. We'd also like to emphasize that the awards reflect the intended results, such as the award for community service is more (or less) important than research, but less (or more) important than the award for quality teaching.

We also recommend highly that an award for the most innovative idea/project also be recognized, **even if the end result was failure**, as it will encourage both faculty and staff to expand their horizons and to develop their creativity. It will also imply that **trust** is still present even if mistakes occur, and that those involved will not be belittled for their efforts and, in fact, they may even enhance their pride-in-workmanship with such "failures."

Case Study: Take a Day Off On Me

A president of a Midwestern college challenges his civil servants by giving a "free" vacation day to any employee whose suggestion results in a task, process or system change. Within one year, vacation days were awarded to six secretaries for suggesting changes in routine forms. The changes resulted in not only an improvement in quality, as tasks were done better and more quickly, but also in reducing the "hassle" factor between staff and management for whom the information was required.

In rewarding and recognizing quality improvement efforts, management should almost always recognize and reward **team efforts** over individual efforts. As Boedecker (p. 191) admirably states: *Group awards, whether at the team, operating unit, or plant level, are also an effective means of improving morale. The feeling of striving toward a common goal, along with the pride of achievement and the memory of the awards ceremony or presentation, will foster a strong sense of group loyalty and identity that will enhance performance over the long term.*

Good recognition and reward programs have the long-term tendency to reduce hierarchy and class distinctions. There are several major reasons for this, namely:

1. An improvement in quality has to be demonstrated before awards can be given to a team or individual. In other words, baseline data has to be freely available.

2. Open communication systems throughout the institution have to be available for all employees. An open-door policy should almost always be the rule, rather than the exception. This includes the right for employees to confront upper management without having the fear of reprisal. (Deming's eighth point: **Drive out fear.**)

When faculty and staff have pride in their work, they become partners in the TQI movement. They become keepers of the inn!

Many unionized colleges and universities use the **contract** as a means to inhibit trust, pride-in-workmanship, and innovation — thus, they actually inhibit the very conditions required to institute quality. It's not unusual for the executive body of the local union to insist that management only exercise "control" over the faculty/staff to the extent permitted in the collective bargaining agreement. In one sense this prevents management from exercising undue power over employees. By the same token, management must then incorporate these limitations into the policies and subsequently into the institution's processes and systems. Since the limitations become part of the processes and systems, bureaucratic controls are the result of control by policy deployment. Control by policy deployment becomes part of the informal mission of the institution and it is much more difficult to change than a traditional institution run by management by objective. Since the collective bargaining agreement can result in control by policy deployment, it can inhibit all conditions necessary to establish quality.

It is important, therefore, that the faculty/staff carefully hold accountable the union leadership for processes and/or systems under the control of the collective bargaining agreement that inhibit employees from having pride-in-workmanship!

Case Study: That's Not in Her Job Classification

At a comprehensive university, the president of the local civil service union noticed that an abnormally high percentage of the secretarial staff in the vice president of development's office was removed from the union's membership roster within 18 months after being hired or transferred into his office. The union president walked in the office and noticed that virtually every civil service employee was performing duties and functions outside of her or his job classification. As a result, she submitted a first-step grievance. The president notified the vice president of development of the grievance and insisted that he inform his staff that they were to work within their job descriptions.

The vice president of development issued a strong memorandum to his staff insisting that they all work only within their job descriptions, and submitted copies to the university and union presidents. But since he never enforced the rule, within a matter of weeks employees were again working outside of their job classifications.

The vice president of development invited the union president for another visit, and again she noticed that staff members were working outside of their job classifications. However, he informed the union president that in spite of his memo, staff members continually worked outside of their job classifications, and asked for her help — the red herring.

After the union president interviewed the staff, she realized the high turnover was attributable directly to promotions within the university and the local community. His office was a training ground for advancement! Furthermore, they were having fun! They were promoted out of the civil service union and thus were removed from the membership roster. The employees informed the union president that if she insisted that they work "by the book," they would elect another president in the next election.

In this case, the union president became an active supporter of empowerment, as long as civil service employees who did not wish to work outside of their job descriptions were not discriminated against. Shortly thereafter, the cumbersome multi-step civil service classification, with the agreement of the union and management, was reduced to three.

Case Study: A Crack In The Old Culture

A medium-size institution was preparing for an accreditation visit. On a previous accreditation review they had been severely criticized for not engaging faculty throughout the campus in the self-study. Responding quickly to this weakness, the president and vice president supported a dean's request for resources to release two faculty members to engage their colleagues in the self-study. Through a series of study groups, committees and sub-committees, people from academic, administrative and student affairs actively participated in preparing the self-study. Meanwhile, they developed ownership in the process, and began to view it as an all-institutional one. Longstanding suspicions of colleagues in other units subsided. At the same time, faculty actively sought means for collaborating with each other in preparing the self-study and other projects. They talked about the quality of programs, students, and advising. The most exciting news was that they began to talk about quality planning, quality control, and quality improvement. Although they were far from changing the institution's culture, they were clearly on the right track, and with the administration's support, they'll be able to influence the course of the institution over time.

Case Study: He Established Pride In Workmanship

Assuming that we had gone through the necessary steps to ensure a quality match between us and the person we select as the new dean of the college of arts and sciences, what steps would you take to establish trust and pride-in-workmanship? This was the question asked of all candidates for the position, since the previous two deans had experienced considerable difficulty in the same position. We had the opportunity to observe the successful candidate over the past several years and we will take this opportunity to share our perceptions.

Step one, day one: The new dean scheduled meetings with each department chair to review enrollments, faculty, curriculum development, budget, and long-range plans. The dean emphasized a philosophy of pre-planning. *We've done this before, and we'll do it again*, became a catch-phrase in the college as the dean emphasized that budget preparation, personnel plans, evaluations, and long-range plans are done every year in predictable cycles. He made it clear that he did not want to hear a department registering surprise that it was time to submit materials related to these yearly obligations.

By focusing on the departments and asking the chairs for their perceptions of strengths and weaknesses, and by demonstrating to them that he knew how academia operated, the new dean quickly adopted a tone of efficiency and regularity for process and systems.

No longer did the chairs and faculty gripe about memos being sent up to the dean's office and lost, or about failing to get an appointment with the dean. Indeed, several were surprised that a call to the dean's office either resulted in an immediate appointment or an immediate return phone call if the dean was not available to field the inquiry. Accessibility and availability soon created a environment of trust among the chairs. They knew that if they registered a concern it would be first of all heard, and if there was something that could be done, it was done. The entire focus was on tasks, processes, and systems — not on people.

In establishing a tone of efficiency, responsiveness, and competence, the new dean ran meetings with precision, wasting no time on trivial matters that were not related to tasks, processes, or systems. He recognized the right of others to speak. He sought to build consensus on issues facing the entire college, and he took a realistic vision of TQM to open meetings with each department. He quickly learned the names of the faculty and early on invited as many as possible to discussion meetings on particular topics. He formed cross-functional teams to address many problems, and he took their suggestions.

Within several months, the new dean began to tackle the depleted morale of his faculty, as he saw they had a great deal of which to be proud. He directed his office to publish regularly the accomplishments of the faculty in the college; he recognized individual faculty for outstanding accomplishments; he organized a highly successful college get-together; he started interdisciplinary faculty committees on pressing social issues, resulting in on-campus workshops and events; he made it clear in his interactions with his peers that he was a spokesperson and advocate for his college and would support it to the fullest.

Assign Quarterly Verbal Reports

One sure fire way to fuse conditions one, two, three, and four is to expect verbal quarterly reports from each TQI council and cross-functional project team. The reports should be formally presented by the chairman of either the TQI council or the project team. In all instances, the entire team should be present for the presentation and the question-and-answer session as well. The reports should address the problem studied and recommendations for eliminating the problem. In all instances, the report should also **recognize success stories**.

It is essential that the president, vice presidents, and deans be present for all reports. In addition, invite faculty, staff, union leadership, and members of the governing board to participate. Be sure to act upon every recommendation or the reporting sessions will become another bureaucratic joke.

All employees — faculty, staff, and administrators — should be recognized formally for their contributions for improving quality. Many corporations have an annual award dinner where recipients are publicly recognized and awards are given to individuals and teams. The awards consist of checks, certificates, pins, plaques, and paid vacations. We encourage colleges and universities to do the same.

Condition Five: Change the Institutional Culture

In the previous sections we elaborated on the necessity to empower employees and students to establish trust, pride-in-workmanship, and quality. Much of the what we promoted can be described as establishing self-leadership skills into the work force, including management. Maximum autonomy and self-leadership are necessary in educational institutions if a culture of excellence is to result. Whereas minimum autonomy will surely result in a quality crisis, maximum autonomy that recognizes the unique talents and contributions of each individual, including students, will lead to positive subcultures based on quality. When quality results are recognized and rewarded, all employees (faculty, staff, and managers) will have an increased pride-in-workmanship, which will result in additional improvements in quality and teaming. This cycle can be so strong that the entire institutional culture may change within five or six years. In fact, Deal and Kennedy (1982) make a case for a strong and unique organizational culture as a necessity for survival and success.

Many institutions of higher education have little knowledge about what they can do to improve quality. Tasks are done in much the same way as they have always been done. Poor faculty performance in the classroom is often tolerated, particularly in unionized settings, because the procedures required to remove lacking individuals are extensive and potentially costly. The proliferation of administrators is often viewed by faculty as management's way of shielding an inefficient administration. Serious grade inflation exists in most of these institutions so that at a typical private college of 2,000 FTE students, fully 30 percent made the dean's list with a minimum 3.5 GPA. At a state university of 6,000 the administration stopped publishing the dean's list because it had grown embarrassingly large. Eventually, the erosion of quality becomes ingrained in the institution's expectations for students, quality instruction, and quality management. As we pointed out in Chapter 2 (please refer to Figure 2.1), certain behaviors yield predictable results, which yield predictable attitudes. This predictable, habitual, unquestioning way of behaving is known as the institution's culture.

The institution's culture can be changed under two conditions. First, when the institution is about to close, and second, when there is a group effort to alter its course. By managing the **systems** towards TQI, the institution's outdated culture is explicitly managed, and thus change is not only possible, it is also probable (please refer to Figure 2.2).

Until **trust and empowerment** are established as routine occurrences, managers, faculty and staff will not readily move toward TQM and TQI. They will resist change, especially in unionized settings, to protect themselves. Such behavior reinforces the old institutional culture. It is apparent, therefore, that even if the entire institution is educated and trained in TQM and TQI processes and systems, little or no change will occur until the trust and empowerment factors are generously woven in the institutional cloth. When this occurs, everyone will be highly supportive of each other's efforts for TQI. As a result, pride-in-workmanship increases and the cycle feeds on itself.

The basic philosophy of every quality leader is based on principles of managing the institutional culture, not the people. Managing does not necessarily mean control. If control is the main agenda of an administration, quality will be difficult to achieve because faculty do not and will not relinquish to a cookie-cutter approach their rights to individual innovation.

Before a new president decides to change the institutional culture, s/he should try to understand how the present institutional culture was established. When either a new institution is started or undergoes a crisis such as retrenchment, there is a formidable discharge of energy from all sectors. Everyone is trying to make the institution a success. Brainstorming, goal setting, cooperation, and innovation exists throughout the entire institution. However, the actions of the president (and to a lesser degree the vice presidents and deans) establish the boundaries and provide important clues as to what the institution will be. Employees notice who and what type of behaviors are rewarded. They also note who leaves or is replaced for not complying with the yet non-official policies. The germination of the institutional culture begins.

At first the institutional culture is quite functional. Most expectations are met. Then as new administrators, faculty and staff are added and as the policies are developed, the institutional culture evolves into distinct segments which are not related to the reward or policy making processes. It is not uncommon for subcultures to exist for managers, staff, and faculty. The institutional culture is no longer managed and almost everyone follows the cultural norms without questioning them, at least, not openly.

Soon after the institutional culture is established, an informal power structure forms to sustain the culture. For example, in an institution that formally expects teaching, research and service from the professors, the

116

informal structure (the institutional culture) may reward only quality research. The actual result is that everybody in the institution begins to believe that it is his/her automatic function to support research for the good of the institution, and by implication, for the good of the state, region, and community.

If a new administrator attempts to change the institutional culture without concentrating on the systems approach toward TQI — establishing trust and promoting empowerment and pride- sin-workmanship — the person's effort will most likely fail. In addition to fearing change, almost all employees require acceptance by their group. As a result, many persons will follow those in charge of the informal power structure since they are the ones who control the retention, promotion, and tenure processes. If the informal power structure is tightly bonded, they may promote a counterculture that can be so powerful as to cause institutional chaos.

Case Study: Changing the Institutional Culture

We are going to show how three different presidents changed the culture of their institution. There are both good and bad points on each attempt.

Case 1: The president in this newly established Western college hired his vice president for academic affairs and his deans based around a central theme of small class sizes and inquiry teaching methods. The first several buildings had classrooms limited to 24 seats. Every laboratory could accommodate only 24 students. Group projects and discussions were encouraged over the traditional lecture method. Core courses and terminal competencies were required of all graduates. All of the newly hired faculty were required to take training in the inquiry method of teaching and in preparing proper course syllabi. Barriers between departments were removed. The culture of innovation and teaming was established as soon as the campus was established.

As time passed and as new administrators came on-board, the traditional lecture method became more prevalent. The newer buildings began to incorporate larger lecture halls. Barriers between the academic departments began to appear. Since most of the science buildings were among the initial structures, the majority of the sciences are still taught in the smaller classes and many of the classes still consist of group projects and inquiry learning. Twenty years later the science graduates of this college continue to be very good.

Case 2: The second president of this very new, highly innovative university in the Midwest hired a new provost/vice president for academic affairs. The new provost took charge and with the consent of the president, changed this university to represent "tradition." Traditional courses replaced modules; course outlines replaced detailed course syllabi; lectures replaced self-instructional modules and discussions; and cost per student credit hour became more important than the student retention rate.

By the time the provost/VPAA left, the administration had replaced the processes and systems that supported innovation with those that supported tradition. Most of the faculty, however, were from the innovation era and were expected to conform to traditional policies. Obviously, a counterculture was established which caused chaos and dissension for nearly 15 years.

Case 3: A newly hired president of this Northeastern institution came aboard during a time of financial exigency. Following the procedures in the collective bargaining agreement he took the necessary actions required to save the institution — he retrenched many faculty. He had to redesign many of the processes and systems, and instituted new policies in a direct, forceful manner. This was required as the institutions was on the brink of failure. Over the next decade he rebuilt the institution to its former strength and led it to financial solvency.

The president, however, still runs the institution as if it is in need of major surgery. He does not promote collegiality. He believes, and has publicly stated, that it his job to determine the direction of the university and that everyone must support his objectives. He constantly threatens people who disagree with either him or his ideas, and has publicly berated not only his closest administrators but also the faculty. He is extremely hierarchial and displays the administrative techniques of Taylorism. As a result, several strong countercultures have emerged: one by the faculty that do everything possible to irritate the president, even at the expense of damaging the educational experiences; and the other by his newly hired administrators who are trying to promote collegiality while they personally seek other positions. This is an example of situational leadership: in times of financial exigency he was truly a leader; in times requiring a vision for quality and consensus, he is not a leader.

In the three cases cited above we have examples of administrators changing their institution's processes and systems to effect a change. We make no judgment whether the changes were desirable (although clearly the third case of saving the institution was preferable); we simply point out that not having the input of those who would be affected by change can cause countercultures to develop.

Ralph H. Kilmann (1985, p. 66) calls the gap between the desired norms and the actual norms within an organization as the "culture gap." The smallest culture gap, according to Kilmann, appears at the top of an organization's hierarchy, whereas the largest culture gap is at the bottom of the hierarchy. This is where, he explains, the lack of trust leads to the we-versus-them attitude found in many organizations.

Closing the culture gap can become a reality when both management and employees work together to alter the tasks, processes, and systems toward quality. For this to occur, administration must empower employees and trust them to form cross-functional teams, and to make constructive recommendations. The administration must manage less and lead more.

Leadership, according to Gardner (1990, p. 1), *is the process of persuasion or example by which an individual (or leadership team) induces a group to pursue objectives held by the leader or shared by the leader and his or her followers.* Gardner says leadership must not be confused with status, power, or authority. This is especially true of colleges and universities where, in our opinion, there has been a lack of leadership over the past several decades. He notes that leaders are part of a system and that they are affected by the system in which they work. Leaders perform tasks that are essential for others to accomplish their purposes, which in this case would be to improve the quality of services and/or product. As quality improves so will the pride-in-workmanship. The end result will be that a new institutional culture will emerge, one in which working becomes fun.

During a recent teleconference, W. Edwards Deming stated that the main reason for working is to have fun. In his book *Joy in Work*, Henri de Man (1939, p. 11) concluded, after interviewing industrial workers in Germany during the mid-1920s, *every worker aims at joy in work, just as every human being aims at happiness.*

U.S. institutions of higher education are at a crossroads in history. Administrators face challenges to traditional ways of managing the quality of programs, faculty, and students. These challenges provide unprecedented opportunities for creative leaders to implement Total Quality Management and Total Quality Improvement programs. Indeed, it's crucial that leaders develop conditions in which TQM and TQI can sustain institutions through critical times of economic and social change.

References

Boedecker, Ray F. *Eleven Conditions for Excellence: The IBM Total Quality Improvement Process*. Boston: American Institute of Management, 1989.

Cornesky, Robert A. et al.*W. Edwards Deming: Improving Quality in Colleges and Universities*. Madison, WI: Magna Publications, Inc., 1990.

Conger, Jay and Rabindra Kanungo. "The Empowerment Process: Integrating Theory and Practice." *Academy of Management Review,* July 1988.

Crosby, Phillip. *Quality Without Tears: The Art of Hassle-Free Management*. New York: McGraw-Hill Book Co., 1984.

Deal, T.E. and A.A. Kennedy. *Corporate Culture*. Reading, MA: Addison-Wesley, 1982.

De Man, Henri. *Joy in Work*. Trans. Eden and Cedar Paul (from the German). London: George Allen & Unwin, 1939.

Deming, W. Edwards. *Out of the Crisis*. Cambridge, MA: Productivity Press or Washington, DC: The George Washington University, MIT-CAES, 1982.

Ferguson, Marilyn. *The Aquarian Conspiracy*. Boston: Houghton Mifflin Co., 1980.

Gardner, John W. *On Leadership*. New York: The Free Press, 1990.

Glasser, William. *The Quality School*. Phi Delta Kappan, 1990.

Hrebiniak, Lawrence G. *Complex Organizations*. New York: West Publishing Co., 1978.

Imai, Masaaki. *Kaizen: The Key to Japan's Competitive Success*. Cambridge, MA: Productivity Press, 1986.

Ishikawa, Kaoru. *Guide to Quality Control*. Englewood Cliffs, NJ: Prentice Hall, 1982.

Juran, J.M. *Juran On Planning For Quality*. Cambridge, MA: Productivity Press, 1988.

Katz, D. and R. L. Kahn. *The Social Psychology of Organizations*. New York: John Wiley & Sons, Inc., 1966.

Kilmann, Ralph H. "Corporate Culture." *Psychology Today,* April 1985.

Levering, Robert. *A Great Place to Work*. New York: Random House, Inc., 1988.

Manz, Charles C. and Henry P. Sims, Jr. *Super-Leadership*. New York: The Berkeley Publishing Group, 1990.

Peters, Tom. *Thriving on Chaos*. New York: Harper & Row, 1988.

Sarazen, Stephen. "The Tools of Quality Part II: Cause-and-Effect Diagrams." *Quality Progress,* July 1990.

Walton, Mary. *The Deming Management Method*. New York: The Putnam Publishing Group, 1986.

Waterman, Robert H. *Adhocracy: The Power to Change*. Knoxville, TN: Whittle Direct Books, 1990.

Total Quality Management Resource Bibliography

Compiled by Susan Ziemba
Center for Business & Industry
Northern Essex Community College
Haverhill, MA 01830
(508) 374-3816
September 1990

Table of Contents

Texts

Crosby, Philip. *The Eternally Successful Organization.* Cambridge, MA: Productivity Press or Cincinnati, OH: Association for Quality and Participation.

——. *Let's Talk Quality: 96 Questions You Always Wanted to Ask Phil Crosby.* Ann Arbor, MI: Masterco.

——. *Quality Without Tears: The Art of Hassle-Free Management.* McGraw-Hill Book Co. or Cincinnati, OH: Association for Quality and Participation.

——. *Quality is Free.* Mentor Books, New American Library.

——. *Running Things: The Art of Making Things Happen.* Cincinnati, OH: Association for Quality and Participation.

Deming, Dr. W. Edwards. *Out of the Crisis.* Cambridge, MA: Productivity Press or Washington, DC: George Washington University, MIT-CAES, 1982; or Methuen, MA: GOAL/QPC.

——. *Quality, Productivity and Competitive Position.* Cambridge, MA: Massachusetts Institute of Technology (MIT-CAES), 1982.

Figenbaum, Armand V. *Total Quality Control.* (3rd ed.) Cincinnati, OH: Association for Quality and Participation or Milwaukee, WI: American Society for Quality Control, 1983.

Gitlow, Howard S. and Shelly J. Gitlow. *The Deming Guide to Quality and Competitive Position.* Prentice Hall or Washington, DC: George Washington University or Cincinnati, OH: Association for Quality and Participation, 1987.

Ishikawa, Kaoru. *Guide to Quality Control.* Prentice Hall, 1982.

Ishikawa, Kaoru and D. Lu. *What is Total Quality Control? The Japanese Way.* Cincinnati, OH: Association for Quality and Participation or Prentice Hall, 1985.

Juran, J. M. *Juran On Planning For Quality.* Cambridge, MA: Productivity Press or Milwaukee, WI: American Society for Quality Control, 1988.

——. *Quality Control Handbook.* (4th ed.) Cambridge, MA: Productivity Press or McGraw-Hill.

——. *Selected Papers.* Juran Institute, Inc.

Juran, J. M., Ed. *Handbook of Quality Control.* McGraw-Hill.

——. *Managerial Breakthrough.* Milwaukee, WI: American Society for Quality Control, 1964.

Juran, J. M. and F. M. Gryna. *Quality Planning and Analysis.* Milwaukee, WI: American Society for Quality Control or McGraw Hill, 1980.

Kilian, Cecelia S. *The World of W. Edwards Deming.* Washington, DC: George Washington University, 1988.

Mann, Nancy R. *The Keys to Excellence: The Story of the Deming Philosophy.* Washington, DC: George Washington University.

Price, Frank. *Right Every Time — Using the Deming Approach.* Milwaukee, WI: ASQC Quality Press.

Ross, Philip J. *Taguchi Techniques for Quality Engineering.* Milwaukee, WI: American Society for Quality Control, 1988.

Scherkenbach, William W. *The Deming Route to Quality and Productivity.* Mercury Press/Fairchild Publications, 1986 or Washington, DC: George Washington University.

Shewhart, Walter A. *Statistical Method from the Viewpoint of Quality Control.* Washington, DC: George Washington University.

Taguchi, Genichi. *Introduction to Quality Engineering.* Uni Publishers and White Plains, NY: Quality Resources.

——. *System of Experimental Design.* Western Electric and White Plains, NY: Quality Resources.

Walton, Mary. *The Deming Management Method.* Dodd, Mead and Co. or Methuen, MA: GOAL/QPC or Cincinnati, OH: Association for Quality and Participation, 1986.

Tools for Planning, Implementing and Continuously Improving with TQM

Aft, Lawrence S. *Productivity, Measurement and Improvement.* Milwaukee, WI: American Society for Quality Control, 1983.

American Productivity Center. *Issues and Innovations: Readings from the American Productivity Center's First Decade.* Houston, TX: American Productivity Center.

ASQC. *Generic Guidelines for Quality Systems.* ASQC, 1979.

ASQC Automotive Division. *Advanced Quality Planning.* Milwaukee, WI: American Society for Quality Control, 1988.

ASQC Quality Costs Committee. *Guide for Reducing Quality Costs.* Milwaukee, WI: American Society for Quality Control, 1987.

——. *Quality Costs: Ideas and Applications.* Andrew F. Grimm, Ed. Milwaukee, WI: American Society for Quality Control, 1984.

——. *The Management of Quality: Preparing for a Competitive Future.* John T. Hagan, Ed. Milwaukee, WI: American Society for Quality Control, 1984.

——. *Principles of Quality Costs.* John T. Hagan, Ed. Milwaukee, WI: American Society for Quality Control, 1986.

——. *Guide for Managing Supplier Quality Costs.* William O. Winchell, Ed. Milwaukee, WI: American Society for Quality Control, 1987.

Barker, Thomas B. *Quality by Experimental Design.* New York, NY: Marcel Dekker, Inc. or Milwaukee, WI: ASQC Quality Press, 1985.

Beckhard, Richard. *Organizational Transitions: Managing Complex Change.* (2nd ed.) Reading, MA: Addison-Wesley Publishing Co.

Belcher, John G. *Productivity Plus: How Today's Best-Run Companies Are Gaining the Competitive Edge.* Houston, TX: American Productivity Center.

Boyett, Joseph H. and Henry P. Conn. *Maximum Performance Management: How to Manage and Compensate People to Meet World Competition.* Cincinnati, OH: Association for Quality and Participation, 1988.

Brassard, Michael. *Memory Jogger Plus.* Methuen, MA: GOAL/QPC.

Buehler, Vernon M. and Y.K. Shetty, Eds. *Competing Through Productivity and Quality.* Cambridge, MA: Productivity Press.

Burke, W. Warner. *Organizational Development: A Normative View.* Reading, MA: Addison-Wesley Publishing Co.

Camp, Robert C. *Benchmarking: The Search for Industry Best Practices That Lead to Superior Performance.* White Plains, NY: Quality Resources.

Caplan, Frank. *The Quality System: A Sourcebook for Managers and Engineers.* Milwaukee, WI: American Society for Quality Control, 1980.

Carrubba, Eugene R. and Ronald D. Gordon. *Product Assurance Principles: Integrating Design Assurance and Quality Assurance.* Milwaukee, WI: American Society for Quality Control, 1988.

Christopher, William F. *Productivity Measurement Handbook.* (Rev.ed.) Cambridge, MA: Productivity Press.

Dixon, George and Julie Swiler. *Total Quality Handbook — The Executive Guide to the New American Way of Doing Business* (compilation). Minneapolis, MN: Lakewood Books.

Dobbins, James H. *Software Quality Assurance and Evaluation.* Milwaukee, WI: ASQC Quality Press.

Doyle, Robert J. *Gainsharing and Productivity: A Guide to Planning, Implementation, and Development.* Cincinnati, OH: Association for Quality and Participation, 1983.

Dudley, James W. *1992 Strategies for the Single Market.* Cambridge, MA: Productivity Press, 1989.

Dyer, William G. *Team Building: Issues and Alternatives.* (2nd ed.) Reading, MA: Addisson-Wesley Publishing Company, 1987.

Egan, Gerald. *Change-Agent Skills.* Two vols. San Diego, CA: University Associates, Inc.

Evans and Lindsay. *The Management of Control and Quality.* St. Paul, MN: West Publishing Co.

Fournies, Ferdinand F. *Coaching for Improved Work Performance.* San Diego, CA: University Associates, Inc.

——. *Why Employees Don't Do What They're Supposed To Do and What To Do About It.* San Diego, CA: University Associates, Inc.

Francis, Dave and Mike Woodcock. *Unblocking Organizational Values.* San Diego, CA: University Associates, Inc.

Fukuda, Ryuji. *Managerial Engineering: Techniques for Improving Quality and Productivity in the Workplace.* Cambridge, MA: Productivity Press or Cincinnati, OH: Association for Quality and Participation, 1984.

GOAL/QPC. *Memory Jogger* (pocket-sized, also in Spanish). Methuen, MA: GOAL/QPC.

——. *Memory Jogger Plus.* Methuen, MA: GOAL/QPC.

Good Measure, Inc. *Solving Quality and Productivity Problems: Good Measure's Guide to Corrective Action.* Milwaukee, WI: American Society for Quality Control.

Greene, James H. *Production and Inventory Control Handbook.* (2nd ed.) Falls Church, VA: APICS, 1986.

Greiner, Larry E. *Power and Organization Development.* Reading, MA: Addison-Wesley Publishing Co.

Griffith, Gary. *Quality Technician's Handbook.* Milwaukee, WI: ASQC Quality Press.

Groocock, John M. *The Chain of Quality: Achieving Market Dominance Through Product Superiority.* Milwaukee, WI: American Society for Quality Control, 1986.

Grossman, Stephen R., Bruce E. Rodgers and Beverly R. Moore. *Innovation, Inc.: Unlocking Creativity in the Workplace.* Plano, TX: Wordware Publishing, Inc.

Hackman, J. Richard and Greg R. Oldham. *Work Redesign.* Cincinnati, OH: Association for Quality and Participation.

Hall, Robert W. *Zero Inventories.* Cambridge, MA: Productivity Press or Milwaukee, WI: American Society for Quality Control, 1983.

Hanna, David P. *Designing Organizations for High Performance.* Cincinnati, OH: Association for Quality and Participation or Reading, MA: Addison-Wesley Publishing Co.

Harrington, H. James. *Poor Quality Cost.* Milwaukee, WI: American Society for Quality Control, 1987.

Hatakeyama, Yoshio. *A Manager Revolution: A Guide to Survival in Today's Changing Workplace.* Cambridge, MA: Productivity Press, 1985.

Hay Research for Management. *Linking New Employee Attitudes and Values to Improved Productivity, Cost and Quality* (research report). Wellesley, MA: Hay Group, Center for Management Research.

Hayes, Glenn E. *Quality Assurance: Management and Technology* (also problem set. Rev. ed.) Milwaukee, WI: American Society for Quality Control, 1983.

———. *Quality and Productivity: The New Challenge.* Hitchcock Publishing Co., 1985 or Milwaukee, WI: American Society for Quality Control, 1985.

Heldt, John J. and Daniel J. Costa. *Quality Pays.* Chicago, IL: Hitchcock Publishing Co.

Imai, Masaaki. *Kaizen: The Key to Japan's Competitive Success.* Cambridge, MA: Productivity Pressor Cincinnati, OH: Association for Quality and Participation, 1986 or Methuen, MA: GOAL/QPC.

Ingle, Sud. *In Search of Perfection: How to Create/Maintain/Improve Quality.* Milwaukee, WI: American Society for Quality Control, 1985.

Ishikawa, Kaoru. *Guide to Quality Control.* Methuen, MA: GOAL/QPC, 1968.

———.*Spanish Guide to Quality Control.* Methuen, MA: GOAL/QPC.

———. *What is Total Quality Control/The Japanese Way.* Methuen, MA: GOAL/QPC.

Japan Management Association, Ed. *Kanban and Just-In-Time at Toyota.* Trans. David Lu. (Rev. ed.) Cambridge, MA: Productivity Press, 1988.

Karatsu, Hajime. *TQC Wisdom of Japan: Managing for Total Quality Control.* Cambridge, MA: Productivity Press, 1988.

King, Bob. *Better Designs in Half the Time, Implementing QFD in America.* Methuen, MA: GOAL/QPC.

———. *Hoshin Planning: The Developmental Approach.* Methuen, MA: GOAL/QPC.

King, Bob Ed. *Implementing Quality Function Development.* Methuen, MA: GOAL/QPC.

Kinlaw, Dennis C. *Coaching for Commitment: Trainer's Package.* San Diego, CA: University Associates, Inc.

Komatsu, Ltd. *QC Handbook.* Cambridge, MA: Productivity Press.

Maass, Richard A. and the ASQC Vendor-Vendee Technical Committee. *World Class Quality: An Innovative Prescription for Survival.* Milwaukee, WI: American Society for Quality Control, 1988.

Maass, Richard A., et al. *Supplier Certification — A Continuous Improvement Strategy.* Milwaukee, WI: ASQC Quality Press.

McLean, Gary M. and Susan H. DeVogel, Eds. *The Role of Organization Development in Quality Management and Productivity and Improvement.* Alexandria, VA: American Society for Training and Development.

Mizuno, Shigeru. *Company-Wide Total Quality Control.* Cambridge, MA: Productivity Press or Cincinnati, OH: Association for Quality and Participation, 1988 or Methuen, MA: GOAL/QPC.

———. *Management for Quality Improvement: The 7 New QC Tools.* Cambridge, MA: Productivity Press, 1988 or Methuen, MA: GOAL/QPC.

Monden, Yasuhiro, Ed. *Applying Just in Time: The American/Japanese Experience.* Cambridge, MA: Productivity Press.

Moran, John W. et al. *A Guide to Graphical Problem-Solving Processes.* Milwaukee, WI: ASQC Quality Press.

Morse, Wayne J., Harold P. Roth and Mary M. Poston. *Measuring, Planning and Controlling Quality Costs.* Milwaukee, WI: American Society for Quality Control, 1987.

Nagashima, Soichiro. *100 Management Charts.* Cambridge, MA: Productivity Press.

Nakajima, Seiichi, Ed. *Introduction to Total Productive Maintenance.* Cambridge, MA: Productivity Press.

O'Grady, P. J. *Putting the Just-in-Time Philosophy Into Practice.* Cambridge, MA: Productivity Press.

Ohno, Taiichi and Setsou Mito. *Just-In-Time for Today and Tomorrow.* Cambridge, MA: Productivity Press.

Pascarella, Perry and Mark A. Frohman. *The Purpose-Driven Organization: Unleashing the Power of Direction and Commitment.* San Francisco, CA: Jossey-Bass, Inc., 1989.

Patton, Joseph D. Jr. *Preventive Maintenance.* Milwaukee, WI: American Society for Quality Control, 1983.

Perry Johnson, Inc. *Design of Experiments I & II.* Southfield, MI: Perry Johnson, Inc.

——. *Problem Solving in the Workplace.* Southfield, MI: Perry Johnson, Inc.

Pfeiffer, J. William, Leonard D. Goodstein, & Timothy M. Nolan. *Applied Strategic Planning: A How to Do It Guide.* San Diego, CA: University Associates, Inc.

——. *Shaping Strategic Planning — Frogs, Dragons, Bees and Turkey Tails.* San Diego, CA: University Associates, Inc.

Porras, Jerry I. *Stream Analysis: A Powerful Way to Diagnose and Manage Organization Change.* Reading, MA: Addison-Wesley Publishing Co.

Russell, J. P. *The Quality Master Plan.* Milwaukee, WI: ASQC Quality Press.

Saaty, Thomas L. *The Quality Master Plan.* Milwaukee, WI: ASQC Quality Press.

——. *Decision Making for Leaders.* Methuen, MA: GOAL/QPC, 1988.

——. *Decision Making: The Analytical Hierarchy Process.* Methuen, MA: GOAL/QPC.

Schein, Edgar H. *Process Consultation. Volume I, Second Edition: It's Role in Organization Development.* Reading, MA: Addison-Wesley Publishing Co.

Schein, Edgar L. *Process Consultation, Volume II: Lessons for Managers and Consultants.* Reading, MA: Addison-Wesley Publishing Co.

Schrock, Edward M. and Henry L. Lefevre. *The Good and the Bad News About Quality.* Milwaukee, WI: American Society for Quality Control.

Shimbun, Nikkan Kogyo/Factory Magazine. *Poke-Yoke: Improving Product Quality by Preventing Defects.* Cambridge, MA: Productivity Press, 1989 or Ann Arbor, MI: Masterco.

Shingo, Shigeo. *Non-Stock Production: The Shingo System for Continuous Improvement.* Cambridge, MA: Productivity Press, 1988.

———. *A Revolution in Manufacturing: The SMED System.* Cambridge, MA: Productivity Press.

———. *The Sayings of Shigeo Shingo: Key Strategies for Plant Improvement.* Productivity Press.

Zero Quality Control: Source Inspection and the Poke-Yoke System. Cambridge, MA: Productivity Press or Cincinnati, OH: Association for Quality and Participation, 1986.

Shores, A. Richard. *Survival of the Fittest: Total Quality Control and Management Evolution.* Milwaukee, WI: American Society for Quality Control, 1988.

Sloan, David and Scott Weiss. *Supplier Improvement Process Handbook.* Milwaukee, WI: American Society for Quality Control, 1987.

Stiles, Edward M. *Handbook for Total Quality Assurance.* National Foremen's Institute, 1964.

Stitt, John. *Managing for Excellence.* Milwaukee, WI: ASQC Quality Press.

Stratton, A. Donald. *An Approach to Quality Improvement that Works: With an Emphasis on the White-Collar Area.* Milwaukee, WI: American Society for Quality Control, 1988.

Suzaki, Kiyoshi. *The New Manufacturing Challenge: Techniques for Continuous Improvement.* Cambridge, MA: Productivity Press.

Talley, Dorsey. *Management Audits for Excellence.* Milwaukee, WI: American Society for Quality Control, 1988.

Tatsume, Sheridan. *The Technopolis Strategy.* Brady Communications, 1986.

Thomopoulos, Nick T. *Strategic Inventory Management and Planning: With Tables.* Chicago, IL: Hitchcock Publishing Co.

Townsend, Patrick. *Commit to Quality.* Cambridge, MA: Productivity Press or Cincinnati, OH: Association for Quality and Participation, 1986.

Wadsworth, Harrison M., Kenneth S. Stephens, and A. Blanton Godfrey. *Modern Methods for Quality Control and Improvement.* Milwaukee, WI: American Society for Quality Control, 1986.

Wallace, Thomas F. *MRPII: Making It Happen.* Falls Church, VA: APICS, 1985.

Walsh, Loren M., Ralph Wurster, and Raymond J. Kimber, Eds. *Quality Management Handbook.* Milwaukee, WI: American Society for Quality Control, 1986.

Walton, Richard E. *Managing Conflict: Interpersonal Dialogue and Third Party Roles.* (2nd ed.) Reading, MA: Addison-Wesley Publishing Co.

Wantuck, Ken. *Just-in-Time for America.* Cambridge, MA: Productivity Press.

Wilkins, Alan L. *Developing Corporate Character: How to Successfully Change an Organization Without Destroying It.* San Diego, CA: University Associates, Inc.

Critical Problem Solving

Adams, James L. *The Care and Feeding of Ideas: A Guide to Encouraging Creativity.* Cincinnati, OH: Association for Quality and Participation, 1986.

Dewar, Jeff. *How to Out-Participate Your Participative Manager and Never Say You're Sorry.* Cincinnati, OH: Association for Quality and Participation, 1986.

Phillips, Steven R. and William H. Bergquist. *Solutions: A Guide to Better Problem Solving.* Cincinnati, OH: Association for Quality and Participation, 1987.

Plunkett, Lorne C. and Guy A. Hale. *The Proactive Manager: The Complete Book of Problem Solving and Decision Making.* Cincinnati, OH: Association for Quality and Participation, 1982.

Van Gundy, Arthur B. *Managing Group Creativity: A Modular Approach to Problem Solving.* Cincinnati, OH: Association for Quality and Participation, 1986.

von Oech, Roger. *A Kick in the Seat of the Pants.* Cincinnati, OH: Association for Quality and Participation, 1986.

―. *A Whack in the Side of the Head.* Cincinnati, OH: Association for
   Quality and Participation, 1983.

Participative Management and Employee Involvement

American Management Association. *Participative Management.*

―.*Productivity and Performance.* American Management Association.

Aubrey, Charles A. and Patricia K. Felkins. *Teamwork: Involving People
   in Quality and Productivity Improvement.* White Plains, NY:
   Quality Resources or Cincinnati, OH: Association for Quality and
   Participation, 1988.

Bain, Lee J. *Statistical Analysis of Reliability and Life-Testing Models:
   Theory and Methods.* Milwaukee, WI: ASQC Quality Press.

Baird, John E. Jr. *Quality Circles Participant's Manual.* Milwaukee, WI:
   American Society for Quality Control, 1982.

―. *Quality Circles Facilitator's Manual.* Milwaukee, WI: American
   Society for Quality Control, 1983.

Barra, Ralph. *Putting Quality Circles to Work: A Practical Strategy for
   Boosting Productivity and Profits.* Milwaukee, WI: American
   Society for Quality Control, 1983.

Barry, Thomas J. *Quality Circles: Proceed With Caution.* Milwaukee,
   WI: American Society for Quality Control, 1988.

Beardsley, Jeff. *Quality Circles: The Management Process.* Cincinnati,
   OH: Association for Quality and Participation, 1984.

Bolman, Lee G. and Terrence E. Deal. *Modern Approaches to
   Understanding and Managing Organizations.* Cincinnati, OH:
   Association for Quality and Participation.

Britannia. *Through the Hoop: Corporate Team Building.* Chicago, IL:
   Encyclopedia Britannica Educational Corporation.

Byham, William C. Ph.D., Jeff Cox. *ZAPP! The Lightning of
   Empowerment.* San Diego, CA: University Associates, Inc.

Crosby, Philip B. *Quality Without Tears: The Art of Hassle-Free
   Management.* Cincinnati, OH: Association for Quality and
   Participation, 1984.

Dinsmore, Paul C. *Human Factors in Project Management.* Cincinnati,
   OH: Association for Quality and Participation, 1984.

Dyer, Constance E., Ed. *The Canon Production System: Creative
   Involvement of the Total Workforce.* Cambridge, MA: Productivity
   Cincinnati, OH: Association for Quality and Participation, 1984.

Dyer, William G. *Team Building: Issues and Alternatives.* (2nd ed.) Reading, MA: Addison-Wesley Publishing Co.

Francis, Dave & Don Young. *Improving Work Groups: A Practical Manual for Team Building.* San Diego, CA: University Associates, Inc.

Gordon, Thomas. *Leadership Effectiveness Training, L.E.T.: The Foundation for Participative Management and Employee Involvement.* Cincinnati, OH: Association for Quality and Participation, 1977.

Grazier, Peter B. *Before It's Too Late: Employee Involvement... An Idea Whose Time Has Come.* Cincinnati, OH: Association for Quality and Participation.

Hall, Jay Ph.D. *Teams and Groups Sampler.* San Diego, CA: University Associates, Inc.

Hastings, Colin, Peter Bixby and Rani Chaudhry-Lawton. *The Superteam Solution.* Brookfield, VT: Gower Publishing Co.

Japan Human Relations Association, Ed. *The Idea Book: Improvement Through Total Employee Involvement.* Cambridge, MA: Productivity Press or Cincinnati, OH: Association for Quality and Participation, 1988.

Jones, John E. *Team Development Inventory-Trainer's Package.* San Diego, CA: University Associates, Inc.

Jones, Louis and Ronald McBride. *An Introduction to Team-Approach Problem Solving.* Milwaukee, WI:ASQC Quality Press.

Lammermeyr, Horst U. *Human Relations — The Key to Quality.* Milwaukee, WI: American Society for Quality Control, 1986.

Maccoby, Michael. *Why Work: Leading the New Generation.* Cambridge, MA: Productivity Press.

Mohr, William L. and Harriet Mohr. *Quality Circles: Changing Images of People at Work.* Cincinnati, OH: Association for Quality and Participation, 1983.

MW Corporation. *Succeeding as a Self-Directed Work Team.* Croton-on-Hudson, NY: MW Corporation.

Phillips, Steven L. and Robin L. Elledge. *The Team-Building Source Book.* San Diego, CA: University Associates, Inc.

Pierce, Richard J. *Involvement Engineering: Engaging Employees in Quality and Productivity.* Milwaukee, WI: American Society for Quality Control, 1986.

Platt, Stephen, Rita Piepe and Judith Smyth. *Teams*. Brookfield, VT: Gower Publishing Co.

Quick, Thomas L. *Inspiring People at Work: How to Make Participative Management Work for You*. Cincinnati, OH: Association for Quality and Participation, 1986.

Reddy, W. Brendan and Kaleel Jamison. *Team Building: Blueprints for Productivity and Satisfaction*. San Diego, CA: University Associates, Inc.

Richey, David. *Getting Results from Employee Participation: Leadership Resource Book*. Cincinnati, OH: Association for Quality and Participation, 1987.

Rubinstein, Sidney P. *Participative Systems at Work: Creating Quality and Employment Security*. Milwaukee, WI: American Society for Quality Control, 1987.

Schmid, John R. *Management by Guts: A No-Nonsense Strategy to Achieve High Quality at Low Cost*. Cincinnati, OH: Association for Quality and Participation, 1985.

Scholtes, Peter R. and contributors. *The Team Handbook: How to Use Teams to Improve Quality*. San Diego, CA: University Associate, Inc. or Madison, WI: Joiner Associates.

Simmons, John and William Mares. *Working Together: Employee Participation in Action*. Cincinnati, OH: Association for Quality and Participation.

Vogt, Judith E. and Kenneth L. Murrell. *Empowerment in Organizations — How to Spark Exceptional Performance*. San Diego, CA: University Associates, Inc.

Weisbord, Marvin R. *Productive Workplaces: Organizing and Managing for Dignity, Meaning and Community*. Jossey-Bass Inc., San Francisco, CA or San Diego, CA: Cincinnati, OH: Association for Quality and Participation, 1988.

Woodcock, Mike. *50 Activities for Teambuilding*. Brookfield, VT: Gower Publishing Co., 1989.

——.*Team Development Manual*. Brookfield, VT: Gower Publishing Co., 1989.

Statistical Process Control,
Reliability and Design of Experiments

Aft, Lawrence S. *Fundamentals of Industrial Quality Control.* Milwaukee, WI: American Society for Quality Control, 1986.

Amsden, Robert, Howard Butler, and Davida Amsden. *SPC Simplified: Practical Steps to Quality.* White Plains, NY: Quality Resources or Cincinnati, OH: Association for Quality and Participation.

ASQC Automotive Division. *Statistical Process Control Manual.* Milwaukee, WI: American Society for Quality Control, 1986.

ASQC Chemical and Process Industries Division. *Experiments in Industry: Design, Analysis and Interpretation of Results.* Milwaukee, WI: American Society for Quality Control, 1985.

ASQC Reliability Division. *Reliability Reporting Guide.* Milwaukee, WI: American Society for Quality Control, 1977.

ASQC Statistics Division. *Glossary and Tables for Statistical Quality Control.* (2nd ed.) Milwaukee, WI: American Society for Quality Control, 1983.

———. *Statistical Techniques How-to Series.* Thirteen booklets. Milwaukee, WI: American Society for Quality Control.

———. *Variables Control Charts.* Milwaukee, WI: American Society for Quality Control.

ASTM. *STP15D/Manual on Presentation of Data and Control Chart Analysis.* Philadelphia, PA: American Society of Testing Materials.

AT&T. *The AT&T Statistical Quality Control Handbook.* Chicago, IL: Hitchcock Publishing Co.

Banks, Jerry. *Principles of Quality Control.* Milwaukee, WI: American Society for Quality Control.

Barker, Thomas B. *Quality by Experimental Design.* Milwaukee, WI: American Society for Quality Control, 1985.

Berger, Roger W. and Thomas H. Hart. *Statistical Process Control.* Milwaukee, WI: American Society for Quality Control, 1986.

Braveman, Jerome. *Fundamentals of Statistical Quality Control.* Cincinnati, OH: Association for Quality and Participation or Milwaukee, WI: American Society for Quality Control, 1981.

Brown, John E. *Statistical Methods in Engineering and Manufacturing.* Milwaukee, WI: American Society for Quality Control Press.

Brush, Gary G. *How to Choose the Proper Sample Size.* Milwaukee, WI: American Society for Quality Control, 1988.

Burr, Irving W. *Elementary Statistical Quality Control.* Milwaukee, WI: American Society for Quality Control, 1979.

———. *Statistical Quality Control Methods.* Milwaukee, WI: American Society for Quality Control, 1976.

Christopher, William. *Productivity Measurement Handbook.* Cambridge, MA: Productivity Press.

Cornell, John A. *How to Apply Response Surface Methodology.* Milwaukee, WI: American Society for Quality Control, 1984.

Diamond, William J. *Practical Experiment Designs.* Milwaukee, WI: American Society for Quality Control, 1981.

Doty, Leonard A. *Reliability for the Technologies.* Milwaukee, WI: American Society for Quality Control, 1985.

Dundan, Acheson. *Quality Control & Industrial Statistics.* Richard D. Irwin, Inc. or Milwaukee, WI: American Society for Quality Control, 1974.

Enrick, Norbert L. with Harry E. Mottley, Jr. *Manufacturing Analysis for Productivity and Quality/Cost Enhancement. Taguchi: Introduction to Quality Engineering.* Uni Publishers, 1983.

Enrick, Norbert L. *Quality Reliability and Process Improvement. (8th ed.) NY: Industrial Press, Inc. 1985.*

Grant, Eugene and R. S. Leavenworth. *Statistical Quality Control. (6th ed.) Milwaukee, WI: American Society for Quality Control, 1980.*

Haaland, Perry D. *Experimental Design in Biotechnology.* Milwaukee, WI: ASQC Quality Press.

Hayes, Glenn E. and Harry G. Romig. *Modern Quality Control.* (Instructor's manual available.) Milwaukee, WI: American Society for Quality Control, 1982.

Hicks, Charles R. *Fundamental Concepts in the Design of Experiments.* Milwaukee, WI: American Society for Quality Control, 1982.

Isikawa, Kaoru. *Guide to Quality Control.* McGraw-Hill, 1974.

Jamison, Archibald. *Introduction to Quality Control.* Milwaukee, WI: American Society for Quality Control, 1982.

Juran, J. M. *Quality Control Handbook.* McGraw-Hill, 1974

———. *Quality Planning and Analysis.* (For engineers.) McGraw-Hill, 1980.

Khuri, Andre L. and John A. Cornell. *Response Surfaces: Designs and Analyses.* Milwaukee, WI: American Society for Quality Control, 1987.

Komatsu Ltd. *Quality Control Handbook: The Seven Basic QC Tools* (pocket-sized). Cambridge, MA: Productivity Press.

Kume, Hitoshi. *Statistical Methods for Quality Improvement.* White Plains, NY: Quality Resources or Cincinnati, OH: Association for Quality and Participation, 1987.

Levin, R. *Statistics for Management.* Prentice-Hall, Inc., 1978.

Lloyd, David K. and Myron Lipow. *Reliability: Management, Methods and Mathematics.* (2nd ed.) Milwaukee, WI: American Society for Quality Control, 1984.

Mason, Robert L. et al. *Statistical Design and Analysis of Experiments With Applications to Engineering and Science.* Milwaukee, WI: ASQC Quality Press.

Messina, William S. *Statistical Quality Control for Manufacturing Managers.* Cambridge, MA: Productivity Press.

Montgomery, Douglas C. *Introduction to Statistical Process Control.* Milwaukee, WI: American Society for Quality Control, 1985.

Nelson, Wayne. *How to Analyze Reliability Data.* Milwaukee, WI: ASQC Quality Press.

———. *Accelerated Testing-Statistical Models, Test Plans, and Data Analyses.* Milwaukee, WI: American Society for Quality Press.

Noreen, Eric W. *Computer-Intensive Methods for Testing.* Milwaukee, WI: American Society for Quality Control, 1985.

O'Connor, Patrick D. T. *Practical Reliability Engineering* (2nd ed.) Milwaukee, WI: American Society for Quality Control, 1985.

Odeh, Robert E. and D. B. Owen. *Parts per Million Values for Estimating Quality Levels.* Milwaukee, WI: American Society for Quality Control, 1988.

Omdahl, Tracy P. *Reliability, Availability and Maintainability Dictionary.* Milwaukee, WI: American Society for Quality Control, 1988.

Ott, Ellis R. *Process Quality Control: Troubleshooting & Interpretation of Data.* McGraw-Hill, or Milwaukee, WI: American Society for Quality Control, 1975.

Perry Johnson, Inc. *Easy as SPC.* Southfield, MI: Perry Johnson, Inc.

———. *SPC Chart Interpretation.* Southfield, MI: Perry Johnson, Inc.

———. *SPC for Short Runs.* Southfield, MI: Perry Johnson, Inc.

——. *SPC for Non-Manufacturing Applications.* Southfield, MI: Perry Johnson, Inc.

Pyzdek, Thomas. *An SPC Primer* (also in Spanish). Milwaukee, WI: American Society for Quality Control, 1984.

——. *Pyzdek's Guide to SPC, Volume 1: Fundamentals.* (Workbook available.) Milwaukee, WI: ASQC Quality Press.

Ryan, Thomas P. *Statistical Methods for Quality Improvement.* Milwaukee, WI: ASQC Quality Press.

Samson, Charles, Philip Hart & Charles Rubin. *Fundamentals of Statistical Quality Control.* Addison Wesley, 1970

Shewhart, Walter A. *Economic Control of Quality of Manufactured Product.* Milwaukee, WI: American Society for Quality Control, 1980.

——. *Statistical Method from the Viewpoint of Quality Control.* Washington, DC: George Washington University. Taguchi, Genichi.

Tufte, Edward R. *The Visual Display of Quantitative Information.* Milwaukee, WI: American Society for Quality Control, 1983.

Western Electric Company. *Statistical Quality Control Handbook.* Milwaukee, WI: American Society for Quality Control, 1956.

Measurement and Evaluation

Hitchcock Pub. Co. *Tools of Metrology.* Chicago, IL: Hitchcock Publishing Co.

Manufacturing Applications

APICS. *Inventory Management Certification Review Course.* Falls Church, VA: APICS.

——. *Production Activity Control Certification Review Course.* Falls Church, VA: APICS.

ASQC Chemical and Process Industries Division Chemical Interest Committee. *Quality Assurance for the Chemical and Process Industries — A Manual of Good Practices.* Milwaukee, WI: American Society for Quality Control, 1988.

Buffa, Elwood S. *Meeting the Competitive Challenge.* Falls Church, VA: APICS, 1984.

Charbonneau, Harvey C. and Gordon L. Webster. *Industrial Quality Control.* Milwaukee, WI: American Society for Quality Control, 1978.

Clampa, Don. *Manufacturing's New Mandate.* Ann Arbor, MI: Masterco.

Dilworth, James M. *Production Observations from Japan.* Falls Church, VA: APICS, 1985.

Edosomwan, Johnson A. & Arvind Ballakur, Eds. *Productivity and Quality Improvement in Electronics Assembly.* McGraw-Hill.

Greene, James H. *Production and Inventory Control Handbook.* (2nd ed.) Falls Church, VA: APICS, 1986.

Hall, Robert W. *Attaining Manufacturing Excellence: Just-In-Time Manufacturing, Total Quality, Total People Involvement.* Cambridge, MA: Productivity Press, 1987 or Cincinnati, OH: Association for Quality and Participation, 1987.

——. *Zero Inventories.* Falls Church, VA: APICS.

Hay, Edward J. *The Just-In-Time Breakthrough: Implementing the New Manufacturing Basics.* Cambridge, MA: Productivity Press.

Hayes, Robert H., Steven C. Sheelwright, and Kim B. Clark. *Dynamic Manufacturing: Creating the Learning Organization.* Cambridge, MA: Productivity Press.

Hirano, Hiroyuki and the JIT Management Laboratory. *JIT Factory Revolution.* Cambridge, MA: Productivity Press.

Huge, Ernest C. *The Spirit of Manufacturing Excellence: An Executive's Guide to the New Mind Set.* Cambridge, MA: Productivity Press.

Laford, Richard J. *Ship-to-Stock: An Alternative to Incoming Inspection.* Milwaukee, WI: American Society for Quality Control, 1986.

Lee, William B. and Earle Steinberg. *Service Parts Management: Principles and Practices.* Falls Church, VA: APICS, 1984.

Lubben, Richard T. *Just-In-Time Manufacturing: An Aggressive Manufacturing Strategy.* Cambridge, MS: Productivity Press or Milwaukee, WI: American Society for Quality Control, 1988.

Maass, Richard A. & the ASWC Vendor-Vendee Technical Committee. *For Goodness' Sake, Help: Two Plays About Quality and the Supplier/Customer Interface.* Milwaukee, WI: American Society for Quality Control, 1986.

Maichryak, Ann. *The Human Side of Factory Automation.* Ann Arbor, MI: Masterco.

Maskell, Brian H. *Just-In-Time Implementing the New Strategy.* Chicago, IL: Hitchcock Publishing Co.

Melnyk, Steve A. et al. *Shop Floor Control.* Falls Church, VA: APICS, 1985.

Ruxton, William E. *Doing Things Right: Managing Quality in the Small Tooling and Machining Company.* Milwaukee, WI: ASQC Quality Press.

Schonberger, Richard J. *Japanese Manufacturing Techniques: Nine Hidden Lessons in Simplicity.* Cambridge, MA: Productivity Press.

———. *World Class Manufacturing Casebook.* Cambridge, MA: Productivity Press.

———. *World Class Manufacturing: The Lessons of Simplicity Applied.* Cambridge, MA: Productivity Press.

Shinohara, Isao. *New Production System: JIT — Crossing Industry Boundaries.* Cambridge, MA: Productivity Press, 1988.

Suzaki, Kiyoshi. *The New Manufacturing Challenge: Techniques for Continuous Improvement.* Cambridge, MA: Productivity Press.

White, John A. *Production Handbook. (4th ed.) Milwaukee, WI: American Society for Quality Control, 1987.*

Service Applications

Albrecht, Karl. *At America's Service: How Corporations Can Revolutionize the Way They Treat Their Customers.* Cambridge, MA: Productivity Press or San Diego, CA: Shamrock Press, 1988.

———. *The Code of Quality Service.* San Diego, CA: Shamrock Press.

———. *Service Within: Solving the Middle Management Leadership Crisis.* San Diego, CA: Karl Albrecht & Associates.

Albrecht, Karl with Steven Albrecht. *The Creative Corporation.* San Diego, CA: Shamrock Press.

Albrecht, Karl and Larry Bradford. *The Service Advantage: How to Identify & Fulfill Customer Needs.* San Diego, CA: Karl Albrecht & Associates.

Albrecht, Karl and Ron Zemke. *Service America! Doing Business in the New Economy.* San Diego, CA: Shamrock Press or Cincinnati, OH: Association for Quality and Participation.

Aubrey, Charles A. II. *Quality Management in Financial Services.* Milwaukee, WI: American Society for Quality Control, 1985.

Carlzon, Jan. *Moments of Truth.* San Diego, CA: Shamrock Press.

Denton, D. Keith. *Quality Service: How America's Top Companies are Competing in the Customer Service Revolution... and How You Can, Too.* Columbia, MD: Boswell Publishing, Inc.

DiPrimio, Anthony. *Quality Assurance in Service Organizations.* Milwaukee, WI: American Society for Quality Control, 1987.

Goldberg, Alvin and C. Carl Pagels. *Quality Circles in Health Care Facilities: A Model for Excellence.* Cincinnati, OH: Association for Quality and Participation, 1984.

Grenier, Robert W. *Customer Satisfaction Through Total Quality Assurance.* Chicago, IL: Hitchcock Publishing Co.

Heskett, James L. *Managing in the Service Economy.* San Diego, CA: University Associates, Inc.

Latzko, William K. *Quality and Productivity for Bankers and Financial Managers.* Methuen, MA: GOAL/QPC, 1968 or Milwaukee, WI: American Society for Quality Control, 1986.

Lefevre, Henry L. *Quality Service Pays.* White Plains, NY: Quality Resources or Milwaukee, WI: ASQC Quality Press.

Rosander, A.C. *Applications of Quality Control in the Service Industries.* Milwaukee, WI: ASQC Quality Press.

——. *The Quest for Quality in Services.* White Plains, NY: Quality Resources.

Shriver, Stephen J. *Managing Quality Services.* East Lansing, MI: The Educational Institute of the American Hotel and Motel Association. 1988.

Townsend, Patrick L. with Joan E. Gebhardt. *Commit to Quality.* Cambridge, MA: Productivity Press.

Zemke, Ron and Carl Albrecht. *Service America.*

Zemke, Ron with Dick Schaaf. *The Service Edge: 101 Companies that Profit from Customer Care.* Minneapolis, MN: Lakewood Books.

Zeithaml, Valerie A. et al. *Delivering Quality Service.* New York, The Free Press.

Military/Federal Government Standards

ANSI/ASQC, A1-1987. *Definitions, Symbols, Formulas and Tables for Control Charts.* Milwaukee, WI: American Society for Quality Control, 1987.

———. A2-1987. *Terms, Symbols and Definitions for Acceptance Sampling.* Milwaukee, WI: American Society for Quality Control, 1987.

———. A3-1987. *Quality Systems Terminology.* Milwaukee, WI: American Society for Quality Control, 1985.

———. B1, 2, 3-1985. *Guide for Quality Control Charts.* Milwaukee, WI: American Society for Quality Control, 1985.

———. C1-1985. (ANSI Z1.8-1971). Milwaukee, WI: American Society for Quality Control, 1985.

———. Q90-Q94 1987 Series. *Quality Management and Quality Assurance Standards.* Milwaukee, WI: American Society for Quality Control, 1987.

———. Z1.4-1981. *Sampling Procedures and Tables for Inspection by Attributes.* (Corresponds to MIL-STD-105D.) Milwaukee, WI: American Society for Quality Control, 1981.

———. Z1-9-1980. *Sampling Procedures and Tables for Inspection by Variables for Percent Nonconforming* (corresponds to MIL-STD-414). Milwaukee, WI: American Society for Quality Control, 1981.

ASQC Energy Division. *Matrix of Nuclear Quality Assurance Program Requirements.* (3rd ed.) Milwaukee, WI: American Society for Quality Control, 1982.

Defense Logistics Agency. *Total Quality Management: A Guide for Implementation.* DoD5000.51-G (pamphlet). Springfield, VA: National Technical Information Service/U.S. Department of Commerce, 1989.

———. *Total Quality Management Master Plan*, (pamphlet). Springfield, VA: National Technical Information Service/U.S. Department of Commerce, 1989.

———. MIL-STD-105D.

———. MIL-STD-414.

The President's Quality and Productivity Improvement Program. *Quality Improvement Prototype.* (Series of pamphlets.) Washington, DC: Office of Management and Budget, 1989.

Robinson, Charles B. *Auditing a Quality System for the Defense Industry.* ASQC Quality Press, Milwaukee, WI.

Educational Applications

ASQC/FICE. *Proceedings of the May 26, 1988 Seminar Proposing a National Educational Quality Initiative,* 1988.

ASQC/FICE/COPA/NCATE. *Summary Proceedings of the Second National Educational Quality Initiative (NEQI) Conference,* 1989.

Fisher, James L. and Martha W. Tack, Eds. *Leaders on Leadership: The College Presidency.* San Francisco, CA: Jossey-Bass, Inc., 1988.

Green, Madeline F. *Leaders for a New Era: Strategies for Higher Education.* New York, NY: Macmillan, 1988.

Harris, John et al. *Assessment in American Higher Education.* Office of Educational Research and Improvement, U.S. Department of Education, 1986.

Harris, John, Susan Hillenmeyer, and James V. Foran. *Quality Assurance for Private Career Schools.* Washington, DC: The Association of Independent Colleges and Schools by McGraw-Hill Publishing Co., 1989.

Ishihara, Shintaro. *Nevertheless, Japan Can Still Say NO.* (Message: bug off, America.)

Matthews, Karl M. *Student Retention and Development: The Creative Service.* The Baxandall Company, Inc., 1988.

Spanbauer, Stanley J. *Quality First in Education... Why Not?* Appleton, WI: Fox Valley Technical College Foundation, 1987.

Motivational Texts Supporting the Need for Total Quality Management in America

Block, Peter. *The Empowered Manager — Positive Political Skills at Work.* San Diego, CA: University Associates, Inc.

Collins, Frank C. Jr. *Quality: The Ball is in Your Court.* Milwaukee, WI: American Society for Quality Control, 1987.

Dertouzos, Michael L., Richard E. Fox. *The Goal.* Falls Church, VA: APICS, 1984 or Cincinnati, OH: Association for Quality and Participation.

Godratt, Eliyahu M. and Robert E. Fox. *The Race.* Falls Church, VA: APICS, 1986.

Guaspari, John. *I Know It When I See It: A Modern Fable About Quality.* Ann Arbor, MI: Masterco or Cincinnati, OH: Association for Quality and Participation.

Harvey, Jerry B. *The Abilene Paradox and Other Meditations on Management.* San Diego, CA: University Associates, Inc.

Karatsu, Hajime. *Tough Words for American Industry.* Cambridge, MA: Productivity Press.

Peters, Tom and Robert H. Waterman, Jr. *In Search of Excellence: Lessons from America's Best-Run Companies.* Video Publishing House.

Popplewell, Barry and Alan Wildsmith. *Becoming the Best.* Chicago, IL: Hitchcock Publishing Co.

Reich, Robert. *The Next American Frontier.* Time Books, 1983.

——.*Tales of a New America.* Methuen, MA: GOAL/QPC, 1987.

Squires, Frank. *Successful Quality Management.* Chicago, IL: Hitchcock Publishing Co.

Managerial Leadership in a Total Quality Environment

American Management Association. *Leadership.*

Bennis, Warren G. *Why Leaders Can't Lead — The Unconscious Conspiracy Continues.* San Diego, CA: University Associates, Inc.

Block, Peter. *The Empowered Manager: Positive Political Skills at Work.* Alexandria, VA: American Society for Training and Development, 1986 or Cincinnati, OH: Association for Quality and Participation.

Drucker, Peter F. *The Frontiers of Management.* Washington, DC: George Washington University.

——.*Management.* New York, NY: Harper and Row, 1974.

Gerstein, Marc S. *The Technology Connection: Strategy and Change in the Information Age.* Reading, MA: Addison-Wesley Publishing Co.

Grayson, C. Jackson and Carla O'Dell. *American Business: A Two Minute Warning — Ten Changes Managers Must Make to Survive into the 21st Century.* Houston, TX: American Productivity Center.

Groolock, John. *The Chain of Quality.* John Wiley, 1986.

Huge, Ernest C. *Total Quality.* Milwaukee, WI: ASQC Quality Press.

Kanter, Donald L. and Philip H. Mirvis. *The Cynical Americans: Living and Working in an Age of Discontent and Disillusion.* San Francisco, CA: Jossey-Bass, Inc., 1989.

Kanter, Rosabeth Moss. *When Giants Learn to Dance: Mastering the Challenges of Strategy, Management, and Careers in the 1990s.* Cincinnati, OH: Association for Quality and Participation, 1989.

Kezsbom, et al. *Dynamic Project Management —A Practical Guide for Managers and Engineers.* Milwaukee, WI: ASQC Quality Press.

Kinlaw, Dennis C. *Coaching for Commitment: Managerial Strategies for Obtaining Superior Performance.* San Diego, CA: University Associates, Inc.

Kouzes, James M., Barry Z. Posner. *The Leadership Challenge: How to Get Extraordinary Things Done in Organizations.* San Francisco, CA: Jossey-Bass, Inc.

Lu, David J. *Inside Corporate Japan: The Art of Fumble-Free Management.* Cambridge, MA: Productivity Press.

Molz, Rick. *Strategic Management: A Guide for Entrepreneurs.* Plano, TX: Wordware Publishing, Inc., 1988.

Monden, Yasuhrio et al. *Innovations in Management: The Japanese Corporation.* Cambridge, MA: Productivity Press.

Morgan, Gareth. *Riding the Waves of Change: Developing Managerial Competencies for a Turbulent World.* San Francisco, CA: Jossey-Bass, Inc.

Nemoto, Maseo. *Total Quality Control for Management: Strategies and Techniques from Toyota and Toyoda Gosei.* Cambridge, MA: Productivity Press.

Ohno, Taiichi. *Workplace Management.* Cambridge, MA: Productivity Press.

Ouchi, William. *Theory Z: How American Business Can Meet the Japanese Challenge.* Cincinnati, OH: Association for Quality and Participation.

Pall, Gabriel. *Quality Process Management.* Prentice-Hall, 1987.

Peters, Tom. *Thriving on Chaos: Handbook for Management Revolution.* Cambridge, MA: Productivity Press.

Umble, Michael M. and M. L. Srikanth. *Synchronous Manufacturing: Principles for World Class Excellence.* Belmont, CA: Wadsworth, Inc.

Case Studies of Companies Using Total Quality Management

Belcher, John G. *Productivity Plus: How Today's Best-Run Companies Are Gaining the Competitive Advantage.* Columbia, MD: Boswell Publishing, Inc.

Denton, D. Keith. *Quality Service: How America's Top Companies are Competing in the Customer Service Revolution... and How You Can, Too.* Columbia, MD: Boswell Publishing, Inc.

Dyer, Constance E., Ed. *The Canon Production System: Creative Involvement of the Total Workforce.* Cambridge, MA: Productivity Press.

Garvin, David A. *Managing Quality: The Strategic and Competitive Edge.* Cincinnati, OH: Association for Quality and Participation or Milwaukee, WI: American Society for Quality Control, 1988.

Goddard, Walter E. *Just-in-Time: Surviving by Breaking Tradition.* Falls Church, VA: American Production and Inventory Control Society, Inc., 1986.

Hall, Robert W. *Kawasaki U.S.A.: Transferring Japanese Production Methods to the United States.* Falls Church, VA: APICS, 1982.

Harrington, H. James. *Excellence: The IBM Way.* Milwaukee, WI: American Society for Quality Control, 1988.

———. *The Improvement Process: How America's Leading Companies Improve Quality.* Cincinnati, OH: Association for Quality and Participation or Milwaukee, WI: American Society for Quality Control, 1986.

Japan Management Association, ed. *Kanban and Just-In-Time at Toyota.* Trans. David Lu. Cambridge, MA: Productivity Press.

Levering, Robert et al. *The 100 Best Companies to Work for in America.* Addison-Wesley, 1984.

Ohno, Taiichi. *Toyota Production System: Beyond Large Scale Production.* Cambridge, MA: Productivity Press.

Schonberger, Richard J. *World Class Manufacturing.* Falls Church, VA: APICS, 1986.

———. *World Class Manufacturing Casebook: Implementing JIT and TQC.* Milwaukee, WI: American Society for Quality Control, 1987.

Shingo, Shigeo. *Study of Toyota Production System: From Industrial Engineering Viewpoint.* Cambridge, MA: Productivity Press, 1981.

General Texts on Organizational Change

American Management Association. *Corporate Culture*. American Management Association.

——. *Managing Change*. American Management Association.

——. *Organization Design & Structure*. American Management Association.

Egan, Gerard. *Change-Agent Skills: Assessing & Designing Excellence: Managing Innovation & Change*. University Associates, Inc.

Glaser, Rollin. *Corporate Culture Survey*. Organization Design and Development.

Jones, Dr. John E., and Dr. William L. Bearley. *Managing Change Assertively*. Organization Design and Development.

——. Organizational Change Orientation Scale (OCOS). Organization Design and Development.

——. *Organizational Change-Readiness Survey*. (OCOS) Organization Design and Development.

Kilman, Ralph H., Teresa Joyce Covin, and associates. *Corporate Transformation: Revitalizing Organizations for a Competitive World.* San Francisco, CA: Jossey-Bass, Inc. Publishers.

Lillrank, Paul and Noriaki Kano. *Continuous Improvement — Quality Control Circles in Japanese Industry.* Ann Arbor, MI: Center for Japanese Studies, University of Michigan.

Locke, Dr. Edwin A. and Dr. Gary P. Latham. *Organizational Goal Setting Questionnaire* (OGSQ). Organization Design and Development.

London, Manual. *Change Agents: New Roles and Innovation Strategies for Human Resource Professionals.* San Francisco, CA: Jossey-Bass, Inc.

Porter, Michael E. *Competition in Global Industries*. San Diego, CA: University Associates, Inc.

Sashkin, Dr. Marshall. *Organizational Beliefs Questionnaire (OBQ)*. (Pillars of Excellence.) Organization Design and Development.

Videos/Films

"Action Plan for Implementing Quality and Productivity." Cambridge: MIT

"Advanced SPC Training: Chart Interpretation." Southfield, MI: Perry Johnson, Inc.

"American Business and Quality." Southfield, MI: Perry Johnson, Inc.

"The AQP Employee Involvement Team Training Program." Cincinnati, OH: Association for Quality and Participation.

"The Art of War: Victory in Business." Boston, MA: Videolearning Resource Group.

"Basic Dimensional Measurement Series." Cleveland, OH: Technicomp.

"Basic SPC Series." Cleveland, OH: Technicomp.

"Before It's Too Late." Atlanta, GA: Thompson Mitchell & Associates, Inc. or Boston, MA: Videolearning Resource Group.

"Beyond Close to the Customer" (with Tom Peters). Atlanta, GA: Thompson Mitchell & Associates, Inc. or Boston, MA: Videolearning Resource Group or Chicago, IL: Films, Inc.

"Building High Performance Teams with Dr. Ken Blanchard" (techniques). Chicago, IL: Films, Inc.

"Building the One Minute Manager Skills." Chicago, IL: Films, Inc.

"Brain Power" (#FY-LEP163). Deerfield, IL: Coronet/MTI Film & Video.

"Burning Question: Losing the Future" (#FY-6085M). Deerfield, IL: Coronet/MTI Film & Video.

"Challenge for the Deming Prize: Total Quality Control in the Service Industry." Washington, DC: George Washington University or Chicago, IL: Encyclopedia Britannica Educational Corporation.

"Change Master Companies: Putting the Theory into Action." (Rosabeth Moss Kanter) Cincinnati, OH: Association for Quality and Participation.

"The Change Masters Program." (Rosabeth Moss Kanter) Cincinnati, OH: Association for Quality and Participation.

"The Change Master: Understanding the Theory." (Rosabeth Moss Kanter) Cincinnati, OH: Association for Quality and Participation.

"Coaching and Counseling: Management Tools for Improving Performance." Cincinnati, OH: Association for Quality and Participation.

"Commitments or Chaos." Chicago, IL: Encyclopedia Britannica Educational Corporation.

"Competing in Time." Chicago, IL: Films, Inc.

"Competing Through Customer Service." Chicago, IL: Films, Inc.

"Competing Through Information Management." Boston, MA: Harvard Business School.

"Competing Through Quality." Boston, MA: Harvard Business School.

"Conflict Management." Salenger, Inc.

"Cost of Quality." Cleveland, OH: Technicomp.

"Creatively Managing Conflicts on Quality Team." Cincinnati, OH: Association for Quality and Participation.

"Crosby on Quality" (strategy & case studies). Chicago, IL: Films, Inc.

"The Customer is Always Dwight" (internal customer). Atlanta, GA: Thompson Mitchell & Associates, Inc. or Boston, MA: Videolearning Resource Group or Chicago, IL: Films, Inc.

"A Day with Dr. W. Edwards Deming on Problems Facing American Industry and Thoughts on Their Solution." Washington, DC: George Washington University.

"A Day with Dr. W. Edwards Deming on Quality and Innovation to Improve Our Economy." Washington, DC: George Washington University, 1988.

"A Day with Dr. Peter F. Drucker (I)." Washington, DC: George Washington University, 1987.

"Deming Library Series" (16 tapes: strategy & application). Methuen, MA: GOAL/QPC or Washington, DC: George Washington University, Chicago, IL: Films, Inc.

"Deming on Quality, Productivity & Competitive Position" (16 videos). MIT.

"The Deming User's Manual" (series; application). Madison, WI: Joiner Associates or Chicago, IL: Films, Inc.

"Deming's 5 Deadly Diseases." Chicago, IL: Britannica.

"Design of Experiments I and II." Southfield, MI: Perry Johnson, Inc.

"Discovering the Future: The Business of Paradigms." (2nd ed.). Chicago, IL: Films, Inc.

"Discovering the Future: The Power of Vision." Chicago, IL: Films, Inc.

"Don't be a Robot" (with Karl Albrecht). San Diego, CA: Shamrock Press.

"Entrepreneurship and Leadership in America." Good Measure, Inc.

"Evaluating and Improving Employee Involvement Teams." Association for Quality and Participation.

"Events at Putnam Creed" (product liability in defective quality). The Glynn Group.

"Excellence in Manufacturing: Vol. 1 Housekeeping Principles." Cambridge, MA: Productivity Press.

"Excellence in the Public Sector." (Tom Peters) Boston, MA: Enterprise Media, Inc. or Boston, MA: Videolearning Resource Group.

"The 14 Steps Management Must Take, I" (Deming). Cambridge, MA: Massachusetts Institute of Technology.

"General SPC Training: SPC in the Manufacturing World." Southfield, MI: Perry Johnson, Inc.

"Girand Series." Methuen, MA: GOAL/QPC.

"Group Action" (organizational change). Interactive video program. Zenger-Miller, Inc.

"Idea Power" (#FY-4876M). Deerfield, IL: Coronet/MTI Film & Video.

"If Japan Can... Why Can't We?" (documentary). Chicago, IL: Films, Inc.

"Imagineering" (#FY-4881M). Deerfield, IL: Coronet/MTI Film & Video.

The "Improving Service" video series (series of eight modules). San Diego, CA: Karl Albrecht & Associates.

"Improving Productivity Through Employee Involvement. Chicago, IL: Encyclopedia Britannica Educational Corporation.

"An Inside Job: Meeting Internal Customer Needs." Chicago, IL: Films, Inc.

"In Search of Excellence: Lessons From America's Best-Run Companies" (stars Tom Peters). PBS Video. Northbrook, IL: Video Arts and Films, Inc. or Chicago, IL: Films, Inc.

"In Search of Excellence, Management Action Program." Northbrook, IL: Video Arts.

"Increasing Productivity." Chicago, IL: Encyclopedia Britannica Educational Corporation.

"Increasing Productivity and Efficiency" (three 22-min. modules). BNA Communications, Inc.

"The Innovator: Producing Powerful Ideas." Chicago, IL: Encyclopedia Britannica Educational Corporation.

"Integrating EI (Employee Involvement) into the Line Organization." Assoc. for Quality and Participation.

"Introduction to Quality Circles." Association for Quality and Participation.

"Inverting the Pyramid: Corporate Performance and Employee Commitment." Chicago, IL: Films, Inc.

"Invitation to Quality Control." Cambridge, MA: Productivity Press.

"Jack Warne's Just-In-Time Video Training Course" (12 videos). Cambridge, MA: Productivity Press.

"The Japanese Do It — Why Can't We?" NBC White Paper. Chicago, IL: Films, Inc.

"Japanese Management in Japan and the United States." ITT Research Institute.

"The Journey to Excellence" (strategy & application). Association for Quality and Participation, Chicago, IL: Films, Inc.

"Juran on Quality Improvement" (16 videos). Wilton, CT: Juran Institute, Inc.

"Juran on Quality Leadership" (strategy). Wilton, CT: Juran Institute, Inc. or Atlanta, GA: Thompson Mitchell & Associates, Inc. or Chicago, IL: Films, Inc.

"Juran on Quality Planning." Wilton, CT: Juran Institute, Inc.

"Just in Time/Just in Case." Videolearning Systems or Chicago, IL: Encyclopedia Britannica Educational Corporation.

"Just-In-Time Production Concepts." General Electric Company.

"The Leader: Encouraging Team Creativity." Chicago, IL: Encyclopedia Britannica Educational Corporation.

"The Leadership Alliance" (with Tom Peters). Atlanta, GA: Thompson Mitchell & Associates, Inc. or Boston, MA: Videolearning Resource Group or Chicago, IL: Films, Inc.

"Leadership on the Shop Floor." Cambridge, MA: Productivity Press.

"Leading the Way." Chicago, IL: Films, Inc.

"Legendary Service." Chicago, IL: Films, Inc.

"Listening Leaders: The Customer Response Loop." Chicago, IL: Films, Inc.

"Ken Wantuck's Just-In-Time for America: An Advanced JIT Implementation Video Course." Cambridge, MA: Productivity Press.

"Management Tools for Improving Performance: Coaching and Counseling." Chicago, IL: Encyclopedia Britannica Education Corporation.

"Management's Five Deadly Diseases" (with Deming). Washington, DC: George Washington University or Chicago, IL: Encyclopedia Britannica Education Corporation.

"Management's Role in Quality Circles." Association for Quality and Participation.

"Managers, Workers and Supervisors Speak Out on the Changing Workplace." Blue Skies Productions or Cincinnati, OH: Association for Quality and Participation.

"Managing Change: The Human Dimension." Good Measure, Inc. or Chicago, IL: Films, Inc.

"Managing Conflict: How to Make Conflict Work for You." Salenger, Inc.

"Managing People Problems Series." (Three videos: "Motivating Employees: Trapped on a Plateau," "Dealing with Different Personalities," and "Are You Really Listening?") Chicago, IL: Encyclopedia Britannica Education Corporation.

"Managing Projects" (method and analysis). Chicago, IL: Films, Inc.

"Managing the Change Process: The Transition State." Good Measure, Inc.

"Managing the Journey" (with Ken Blanchard). Atlanta, GA: Thompson Mitchell & Associates, Inc. or Chicago, IL: Films, Inc.

"Masters Statistical Process Control." Cleveland, OH: Technicomp.

"Measuring Team Activities." Association for Quality and Participation.

"Meetings Bloody Meetings" (stars John Cleese). Resource Presentations.

"Meetings: Isn't There a Better Way?" 16 mm film, 1981. VISUCOM Productions, Inc.

"Megatrend." Thompson Mitchell Associates.

"Mental Floss and Mirthquakes" (creative participative techniques). Cincinnati, OH: Association for Quality and Participation.

"Michael Porter on Competitive Strategy." Boston, MA: Harvard Business School.

"Moments of Truth" (with Connie Selleca). San Diego, CA: Karl Albrecht & Associates or Shamrock Press.

"Motivation and Productivity: We Learn from the Japanese." Encyclopedia Britannica Education Corporation.

"MRP Starter Set." Milwaukee, WI: The Forum Ltd.

"The New Manufacturing Challenge: Techniques for Continuous Improvement." Cambridge, MA: Productivity Press.

"The New Partnership: Managing for Excellence with Tom Melohn." Chicago, IL: Films, Inc.

"Organizational Development for Improved Productivity." Harris Corporation.

"Overcoming Resistance to Employee Involvement." Cincinnati, OH: Association for Quality and Participation.

"Participative Management: We Learn from the Japanese." Chicago, IL: Encyclopedia Britannica Education Corporation.

"A Passion for Customers" (with Tom Peters). Des Plaines, IL: Video Publishing House or Films, Inc.

"A Passion for Excellence" (with Tom Peters). Short or complete version. Des Plaines, IL: Video Publishing House or Films, Inc.

"People and Productivity: We Learn from the Japanese." Chicago, IL: Encyclopedia Britannica Education Corporation.

"Planning a Project and Building Your Project Team." Chicago, IL: Encyclopedia Britannica Education Corporation.

"The Poke-Yoke System." Video or slides. Cambridge, MA: Productivity Press.

"Popping the Balloons: 13 Myths and Realities about Participative Management." Association for Quality and Participation.

"Power of the Suggestion System." Cambridge, MA: Productivity Press.

"Problem Solving." Cleveland, OH: Technicomp.

"Problem Solving — A Process for Managers." Chicago, IL: Encyclopedia Britannica Education Corporation.

"Problem Solving in the Workplace." Southfield, MI: Perry Johnson, Inc.

"Process Control for Short Production Runs." Cleveland, OH; Technicomp or Boston, MA: Videolearning Resource Group.

"Productivity and the Self-Fulfilling Prophecy: The Pygmalion Effect." McGraw-Hill Training Systems.

"Productivity Payoff." Learning Corporation of America.

"Project Management Series." Chicago, IL: Encyclopedia Britannica Educational Corporation.

"Pursuit of Efficiency." Atlanta, GA: Thompson Mitchell & Associates, Inc.

"Quality and Productivity in Service Organizations" (Deming). Cambridge, MA: Massachusetts Institute of Technology.

"Quality Circles: For My Own Cause." Chicago, IL: Encyclopedia Britannica Educational Corporation.

"The Quality Connection" (John Guaspari, service and manufacturing). Atlanta, GA: Thompson Mitchell & Associates, Inc. or Boston, MA: Videolearning Resource Group or Chicago, IL: Films, Inc.

"Quality Engineering Design: Introduction to the Taguchi Approach." Rochester, NY: Rochester Institute of Technology.

"Quality Function Deployment." Cleveland, OH: Technicomp.

"Quality in the 21st Century" (Philip Crosby, 10 volumes of case studies). Boston, MA: Videolearning Resource Group or Chicago, IL: Films, Inc.

"The Quality Man" (Philip Crosby, strategy). Also in Spanish. Cincinnati, OH: Association for Quality and Participation, or Chicago, IL: Films, Inc.

"Quality Planning" (10- to 30-minute modules). Society of Manufacturing Engineers.

"The Quality Revolution" (#FY-5971M). Deerfield, IL: Coronet/MTI Film & Video.

"Quest for Quality." Boston, MA: Videolearning Resource Group.

"Remedies for Faulty Practices of Management: Theory is in Hand for Better Management." Washington, DC: George Washington University.

"Roadmap for Change (Part I): The Deming Approach." Washington, DC: George Washington University or Chicago, IL: Encyclopedia Britannica Educational Corporation.

"Roadmap for Change (Part II): The Deming Legacy." Washington, DC: George Washington University of Chicago, IL: Encyclopedia Britannica Educational Corporation.

"Roadmap for Change (Part III): Commitment to Quality." Atlanta, GA: Thompson Mitchell & Associates, Inc. or Chicago, IL: Encyclopedia Britannica Educational Corporation.

"Roadmap for Change: Pontiac Fiero." Encyclopedia Britannica Educational Corporation.

"Rosabeth Moss Kanter on Synergies, Alliances and New Ventures." Boston, MA: Harvard Business School.

"The Safety Secret." Chicago, IL: Films, Inc.

"Self-Directed Work Teams: Redesigning the Workplace for the 21st Century." Cincinnati, OH: Association for Quality and Participation or Boston, MA: Videolearning Resource Group.

"Self-Managing Work Force Saves Money and Jobs." Cincinnati, OH: Association for Quality and Participation.

"Service Excellence" (six 15-minute modules). Chicago. IL: Films, Inc.

"Service Management" (with Karl Albrecht). San Diego, CA: Karl Albrecht & Associates or Shamrock Press.

"Service Strategy" (with Robert Guillaume). San Diego, CA: Karl Albrecht & Associates or Shamrock Press.

"Service Within" (with Karl Albrecht). San Diego, CA: Karl Albrecht & Associates.

"Shape of the Winner" (Tom Peters). Boston, MA: Videolearning Resource Group or Des Plaines, IL: Video Publishing House or Chicago, IL: Films, Inc.

"The SMED System." Video or slides. Cambridge, MA: Productivity Press.

"SPC for Non-Manufacturing Applications." Southfield, MI: Perry Johnson, Inc.

"SPC for Short Runs." Southfield, MI: Perry Johnson, Inc.

"SPC Implementation." Southfield, MI: Perry Johnson, Inc.

"Statistical Process Control" (11 modules). GMI Engineering & Management Institute.

"Statistical Process Control — SPC Basic Series and SPC II: Master Series." Boston, MA: Videolearning Resource Group or Cleveland, OH: Technicomp.

"Stew Leonard: Creating the Customer's Dream." Chicago, IL: Films, Inc.

"The Supervisor-Motivating Through Insight." Chicago, IL: Films, Inc.

"Sustaining Quality Circles." Cincinnati, OH: Association for Quality and Participation.

"Taguchi Approach to Quality Optimization." Cleveland, OH: Technicomp.

"Taking the Challenge." Chicago, IL: Films, Inc.

"Talking To the Team: How To Run A Team Meeting." Boston, MA: Videolearning Resource Group.

"Teambuilding." McGraw-Hill Training Systems.

"Team Building: An Exercise in Leadership." Columbia, MD: Boswell Publishing, Inc.

"Team Excellence" (methods for management). Chicago, IL: Films, Inc.

"Thriving on Chaos" (with Tom Peters). Atlanta, GA: Thompson Mitchell & Associates, Inc. or Des Plaines, IL: Video Publishing House.

"Through the Hoop: Corporate Team Building." Chicago, IL: Encyclopedia Britannica Educational Corporation.

"Time on the Line." Chicago, IL: Encyclopedia Britannica Educational Corporation.

"Total Quality Control: An Open Secret to Success." Chicago, IL: Encyclopedia Britannica Educational Corporation.

"Towards Excellence With Tom Peters." Zenger-Miller, Inc.

"TQC: The Customer, The Process, The Data." Cincinnati, OH: Association for Quality and Participation or Atlanta, GA: Thompson Mitchel & Associates, Inc. or Chicago, IL: Encyclopedia Britannica Educational Corporation.

"TQC/Manufacturing: The Customer, The Process, The Data." Cincinnati, OH: Association for Quality and Participation or Boston, MA: Videolearning Resource Group or Chicago, IL: Encyclopedia Britannica Educational Corporation.

"TQC/Service: The Customer, The Process, The Data." Chicago, IL: Encyclopedia Britannica Educational Corporation. "Trust Your Team" (participative management). Chicago, IL: Films, Inc.

"We're On The Same Team, Remember?" (motivation). Chicago, IL: Films, Inc.

"What Have You Changed Lately? Managing for Innovation in Health Services." Palo Alto, CA: TPG Communications.

"What You Are is Where You Were When" (values, prejudice & reacting to change). Chicago, IL: Films, Inc.

"What's Quality Got to Do With It?" (service quality improvement). Atlanta, GA: Thompson Mitchell & Associations, Inc. or Boston, MA: Videolearning Resource Group.

"When You See It, You Know it."

"Who's Responsible?" Chicago, IL: Encyclopedia Britannica Educational Corporation.

"Why Productivity Increases as Quality Improves" (Deming). Cambridge, MA: Massachusetts Institute of Technology.

"Why Quality?" (service & manufacturing). Chicago, IL: Films, Inc.

"Win With Teamwork" (motivation). Chicago, IL: Films, Inc.

"Work Worth Doing" (case studies). Boston, MA: Videolearning Resource Group or Chicago, IL: Films, Inc.

"Working Through Quality Circles at Hewlett-Packard." Cincinnati, OH: Association for Quality and Participation.

"Working Together." Chicago, IL: Encyclopedia Britannica Educational Corporation.

"Working Together Through Employee Participation Circles." Lockheed-California Company.

"Working Together Works!" Chicago, IL: Films, Inc.

"A World Turned Upside Down." Des Plaines, IL: Video Publishing House.

"Why Quality?" (based on John Guaspari). Atlanta, GA: Thompson Mitchell & Associates, Inc.

Audio Cassette Series

"Effective Team Building" (14 tape series with Brian Tracy). Boston, MA: Videolearning Resource Group.

"The Skills of Appraisal" (tape and working manual). Brookfield, VT: Gower Publishing Co.

Magazines and Newsletters

Competitive Times. Methuen, MA: GOAL/QPC.

HRD Quarterly. Organization design and development. King of Prussia, PA 1940 or Greensboro, NC: Center for Creative Leadership.

Journal for Quality and Participation. Cincinnati, OH: Association for Quality and Participation.

Organizational Dynamics. New York, NY: American Management Association.

Quick Changeover User Group Newsletter. Norwalk, CT: Productivity, Inc.

Production and Inventory Management Journal. American Production and Inventory Control Society, Inc., 500 West Annadale Road, Falls Church, VA 22046-4274.

Productivity Newsletter. Cambridge, MA: Productivity Press.

Quality Progress.

Quality Speaks. Appleton, WI: The Academy for Quality in Education.

The Service Edge Newsletter. Minneapolis, MN: Lakewood Publications.

Service Insider. Cambridge, MA: Productivity Press.

Total Employee Involvement TEI Newsletter. Cambridge, MA: Productivity Press.

Total Quality Newsletter. Minneapolis, MN: Lakewood Publications.

Total Quality Management Journal. Carfax Publishing Company, 85 Ash St., Hopkinton, MA 01748.

Bibliographies

American Productivity Center. *Focus* (audiovisual aides for quality/quality work life). Houston, TX: American Productivity Center.

Holt, Kathleen, Ed. *Implementing Innovation: An Annotated Bibliography.* Greensboro, NC: Center for Creative Leadership, 1987.

Howell, Vincent. *Quality Improvement Through Continuing Education: An Engineer's Guide for Life-Long Learning* (directory of schools/programs). Milwaukee, WI: American Society for Quality Control, 1986.

Johnson, George A. *APICS Bibliography* (production and inventory management and related subjects). Falls Church, VA: APICS.

Krismann, Carol. *Quality Control — An Annotated Bibliography to 1988.* White Plains, NY: Quality Resources.

Ziemba, Susan. *Total Quality Management Resource Bibliography.* Haverhill, MA: Northern Essex Community College. 1990.